Henrietta Warleigh

Full directions for knitting socks : stockings, babies', code, doll's and seamen's things etc., over 430 patterns, sizes and sorts

Henrietta Warleigh

Full directions for knitting socks : stockings, babies', code, doll's and seamen's things etc., over 430 patterns, sizes and sorts

ISBN/EAN: 9783743399969

Manufactured in Europe, USA, Canada, Australia, Japa

Cover: Foto ©ninafisch / pixelio.de

Manufactured and distributed by brebook publishing software (www.brebook.com)

Henrietta Warleigh

Full directions for knitting socks : stockings, babies', code, doll's and seamen's things etc., over 430 patterns, sizes and sorts

No. 1.

FULL DIRECTIONS AND SCALES

FOR

KNITTING SOCKS.

Stockings, Babies, Doll's, Doll's and Seamen's things, Etc.

OVER 430 PATTERNS, SIZES AND SORTS.

BY

HENRIETTA WARLEIGH

AUTHORESS OF

[illegible]

AND

[illegible]

SEVENTH EDITION, VERY MUCH ENLARGED.

SIMPKIN, MARSHALL, HAMILTON, KENT & Co.

IX, Paternoster Row, London

[illegible]

PRICE ONE SHILLING

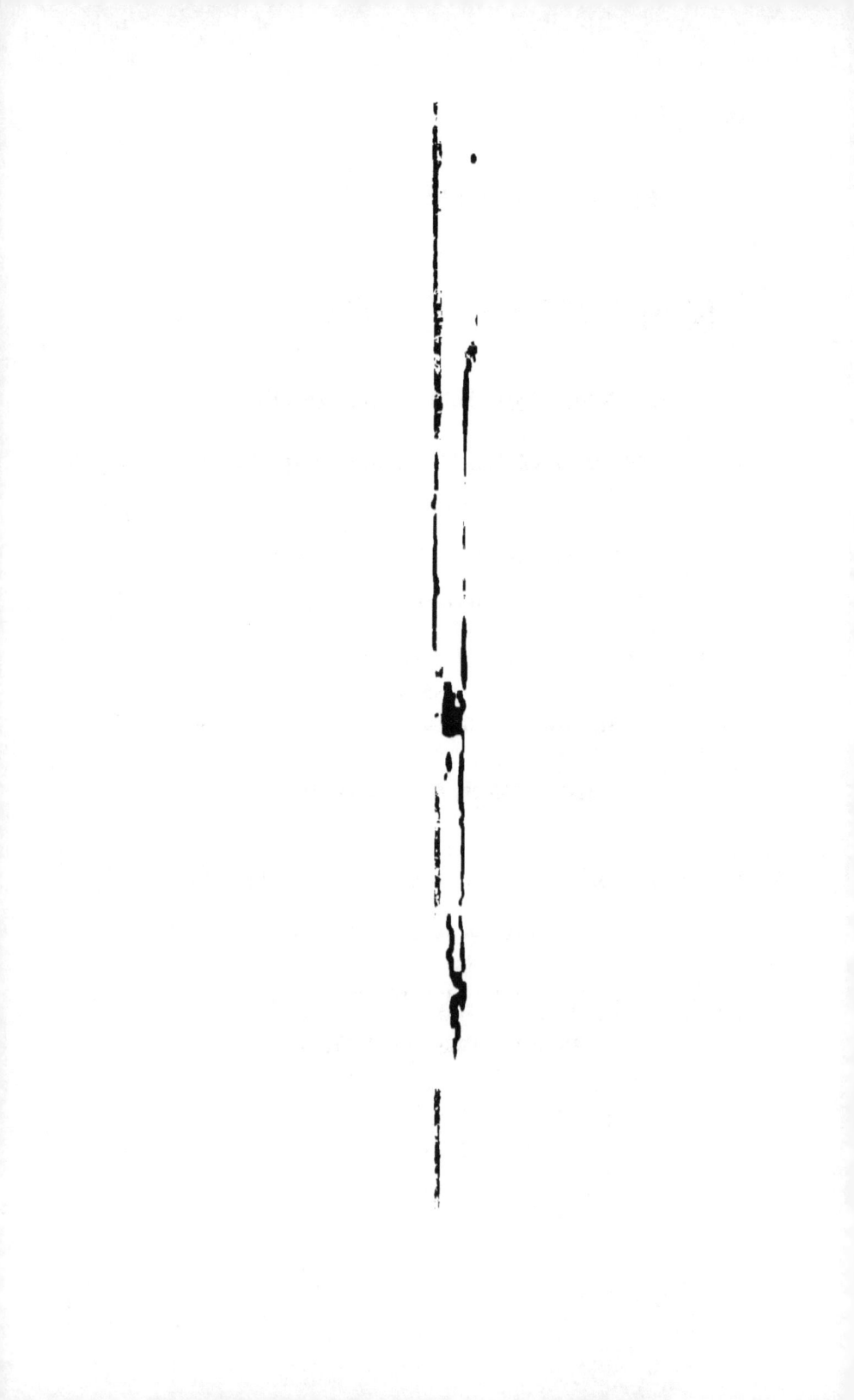

No. 1.

FULL DIRECTIONS AND SCALES

FOR

KNITTING SOCKS,

Stockings, Babies', Code, Doll's and Seamen's things, Etc.,

OVER 430 PATTERNS, SIZES AND SORTS.

BY

HENRIETTA WARLEIGH.

AUTHORESS OF

No. 2. Full Directions and Scales for Knitting Gloves, etc.

AND

No. 3. Full Directions for Knitting over 140 Edgings, Circles, etc.

SEVENTH EDITION, VERY MUCH ENLARGED.

1894

SIMPKIN, MARSHALL, HAMILTON, KENT & Co.,

32, PATERNOSTER ROW, LONDON.

ALL RIGHTS RESERVED.

PRICE ONE SHILLING.

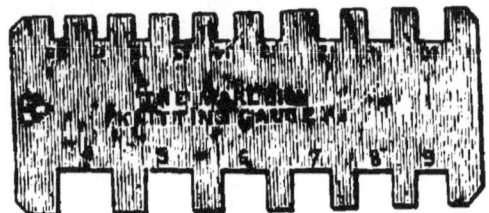

PRESS NOTICES ON No. 1.

"Through the medium of this book a complete knowledge of knitting may be acquired."—*Liverpool Weekly Albion.*

"The success of the work is a sufficient guarantee of its merits."—*School Board Chronicle.*

"We recommend it as extremely useful."—*Myra's Journal.*

"It is comprehensive in range, neat in style, and most useful and necessary in its object."—*Tewksbury Record.*

"This appears to be a useful guide for the very useful occupation with which it deals."—*Woman's Work.*

"This book is a marvel of ingenuity, a great boon to the knitting world"—*Liverpool Daily Courier.*

"The book is a practical one, and with its help the art of knitting articles of every description, and of every possible size, is reduced to a simple method by means of scales which a child would not fail to understand."—*Daily Post.*

"Sufficient testimony is borne to the value of this book by the fact that it is now in the seventh edition."—*School Guardian.*

"The leading feature in this book is that one set of directions is given, and a scale appended, whereby a similar article of every useful size can be made. It is to be hoped that its undoubted merits will obtain for it the wide circulation it deserves."—*Oxford Times.*

"The information is reliable and the directions are plainly expressed."—*Schoolmaster.*

"A vast amount of time and pains has been taken to ensure correct proportions; the book is well worth the commendation it has received."—*Schoolmistress.*

"Never have we met with a manual including directions so varied in such a small compass. Many of the patterns have been tried by a little girl, who has worked from them without difficulty—a forcible proof of the conciseness and accuracy of the receipts which have been lavished on most subjects."—*The Queen.*

"The London School Board have adopted this book—a strong recommendation in its favour."—*Hertfordshire Mercury.*

"It has been found specially useful in teaching knitting to School children."—*Woman's Gazette.*

"A great feature is its graduated scales."—*Hampshire Independent.*

"By following the instructions exactness in shape may be ensured."—*Rock*.

"The musical drill has proved very successful in promoting regularity and rapidity of work."—*Health Journal*.

"The precise yet plainly stated directions can be easily mastered and the most elaborate articles successfully worked. The practical nature of the work ensures a complete knowledge of the valuable art."—*Essex Telegraph*, on No. 4.

"The directions are given in a very clear manner."—*Hertfordshire Mercury*, on Nos. 2 and 3.

"The great advantage of the principle in these books is that when one article has been made, it is easy to produce it in several sizes."—*Sussex Coast Mercury*, on Nos. 1 and 2.

"The instructions are very clear and simple."—*School Board Chronicle*; second notice on Nos. 1, 2 and 3.

"As they supply precise details and figures, these books put it within the power of anyone to execute the most ambitious pieces of work."—*The Scotsman*, on Nos. 1, 2 and 3.

"By a careful study of Miss WARLEIGH's excellent handbooks, ladies may soon learn to make a great variety of useful articles at a comparatively small cost."—*The Courant*, on Nos. 1, 2 & 3.

"The scientific scales reduce the complicated art of knitting a stocking or vest to a simple concise method."—*Daily Post*, second notice on Nos. 1, 2 and 3.

"These useful manuals are written by Miss WARLEIGH, who cannot be too highly complimented on the ingenuity and exactness displayed in their production."—*The Queen*, second notice on Nos. 1, 2 and 3.

"These manuals appear to us to be concise and well adapted for educational purposes."—*Health* on Nos. 1, 2 and 3.

"All lovers of knitting have good reason to be grateful to Miss WARLEIGH for her very excellent series of books, to which it is really a pleasure to call the attention of our readers."—*The Lady*, second notice on Nos. 1, 2 and 3.

And many other favourable notices of all the books, from well known knitters, directresses of needlework, head teachers, etc. Nos. 1 and 2 are used in Whiteland's Training College and several others.

CONTENTS.

The things marked thus * are new in this edition.

	PAGE.
Abbreviations, 2	9
Advantages of knitting, 6	2
Antimacassars, 3	42
Appropriation of yarns	6
Asterisk	3
Babies' boots, 6 sorts, each in 3 or 4 sizes	61
* Ditto, No. 1, 2 scales, each of 4 sizes	83, 84
* Ditto, No. 2, 2 scales, each of 4 sizes	85, 86
Babies' first socks, 6 sizes	46
Babies' gloves, 2 sorts	36
Ditto, double scale of 6 sizes each	87
Babies' leggings	46
Ditto, scale of 3 sizes	88
Babies' vests, 4 sorts, each in 3 sizes	27
Balls, 2 sizes	39
Bath or washing gloves	32
Ditto, scale of 6 sizes	87
Bath or washing squares, 3 sorts and sizes	32
Bath or washing towels, 3 sorts and sizes	42
Blackboard rubbers, 2 sizes	33
*Boating cap	47
Bootakins, 2 sorts	50
Ditto, No. 1, in rounds, scale of 4 sizes	97
* Ditto, No. 2, in rows, scale of 4 sizes	86
*Braces, 2 sizes	46
Canadian gloves	47
Casting on and casting off, 2 ways	22
Casting off double	17
Chain edge	23
Chest wraps or crossovers	38
Ditto, scale of 6 sizes	85
*Classification of yarns, 7 classes	5
*Clocks or Clox, knitted in	80
Code knitting	24
Combined cuffs and mittens, all sizes	32
Comforters, 3 sorts	45
Ditto, scale of 6 sizes	88
Corals or gimps, 3 sorts	51
Cuffs, 9 sorts	43
Ditto, scale of 8 sizes	95
*Derivation and history of knitting	1
Divided foot, all sizes	17

*Divided gusset knee, all sizes	74
*Dolls' boots, 4 sorts	61
Ditto, No. 1, 2 scales of 2 and 3 sizes 83,	84
Ditto, No. 2, 2 scales, each of 4 sizes 85,	86
*Dolls' bootakins, 2 sizes and sorts 50,	82
Ditto, scale of 2 sizes	86
Dolls' cuffs, 4 sorts 25,	26
Dolls' hoods, 2 sorts 52,	78
Ditto, No. 2, scale of 3 sizes	96
*Dolls' muffs, 2 sizes	51
*Dolls' stays	19
Ditto, scale of 3 sizes	89
*Dolls' Tam o' Shanters, 2 sizes	73
*Dolls' vests, 4 sizes and sorts	34
Ditto, scales 90, 91, 92,	93
Dolls' socks	11
Ditto, scale of 4 sizes	97
*Double cuffs, all sizes	44
Drill for knitting and purling	21
Dusters, 2 sizes and sorts	48
*Fancy work cuffs, all sizes	44
Fancy work hose, all sizes	19
*Floor rubbers, 3 sizes	33
Frilled cuffs, all sizes	43
*Frilled edge cuffs, all sizes	44
Fringes, 6 sorts, for all purposes	39
*Furrow in heel flap	80
Garters	38
Garter work	2
Gauge for needles and pins	ii.
*Grafting	77
*Gusset knee, in rows, all sizes	74
*Gusset knee, in rounds, all sizes	53
Hand mufflers or Canadian gloves	47
Ditto, scale of 6 sizes	87
Hem for top of hose, 2 ways	11
*Hip gusset, in rows, all sizes	49
Hoods, 3 sorts	52
No. 1, Square, in 3 sizes	52
No. 2, Horseshoe, scale of 6 sizes	95
No. 3, Triangle, in 3 sizes	78
Horseshoe or Dutch heel, all sizes	13
*Hyphens	9
Joining yarn, maxim 12	23
Kettle or iron holders, 2 sorts, each in 2 sizes	41
*Kilted cuffs	44
Knee caps, 2 sorts	60
Ditto, No. 1, in rows, scale of 8 sizes	89

*Knee caps, No. 2, in rounds, 2 sizes	60
Knitting for beginners	9
*Knitting for invalids	10
Knitting stitch and drill	21
Knitting that may be cut	51
Laundry blue bags, 2 sizes	33
Leggings	39
Ditto, scale of 6 sizes	88
Long socks or 3/4 hose	11
Ditto, scale of 11 sizes	97
Loop garter	38
Loose heel, all sizes	14
Made stitches, 3 ways	7
Manufacturers toe, all sizes	16
Maxims for knitters, 18	22
Mittens, with thumbs and gussets	30
Ditto, scale of 11 sizes	94
*Money or sample bags, 2 sizes	33
*Muffs, 2 sizes	51
Music for drill	20
Neckties, 2 sorts, each in 2 sizes	18
Needles and pins	3
Night caps, 2 sorts, each in 2 sizes	47
Night or sleeping socks	48
Ditto, scale of 4 sizes	97
Oranges, for Christmas trees, 2 sizes	39
*Ornamental chest for vest 3	81
*Ornamental top for hose, all sizes	80
*Over	9
Patchwork shapes, 4 sorts, each in 2 sizes	40
Pence jug	72
Pupil teachers' knitting	27
Purling stitch and drill	21
Ribbed hose, all sizes	18
*Ribbon holes in frilled edge cuffs	81
Ribs	8
Ridges	7
R.H.N. and L.H.N.	9
*Rig and fur hose, all sizes	13
*Repeating designs, 17, in rows and rounds	54
No. 2, Annaberg, rounds	54
No. 1, Barbara, rows	54
No. 11, Bee, rows	56
No. 3, Brioche, rows	54
No. 10, Clerica, 2 parts, rows	56
No. 17, Clio, rounds	81
No. 14, Diamond, 5 sizes, rows	57
No. 12, Doric, rounds	56

* No. 6, Hemstitch, 5 sizes, rows	55
* No. 13, Hollingsclough, 2 parts, rows and rounds	57
No. 4, Huckaback, 4 sizes, rows	54
No. 15, Kilt, 4 sizes, each in 2 parts, rounds	58
* No. 7, Phœbe, rows	55
* No. 5, Roma, 2 sizes, rows	55
* No. 8, Spira, 2 parts, rounds	55
No. 9, Wave, rounds	56
* No. 16, Melrose, rows	59
*Scale and shop size	82
*Seamen's knitting, 7 articles	79
*Selection of implements and yarns	6
*Sexagon cuffs, all sizes	81
*Shields or chest and throat protectors	75
Silk hose, all sizes	11
Skull caps or zucchettas, 5 sorts	28
Slate rubbers, 2 sizes	27
Socks or ½ hose	11
Ditto, scale of 11 sizes	97
*Spaced comforters, all sizes	45
*Stays for children, with gussets	49
* Ditto, scale of 6 sizes	89
Stitch and row metre	8
Stockings or hose	11
Ditto, scale of 11 sizes	97
Stocking work	2
*Strengthening the knee	74
Strengthening the heel	13
Strengthening the toe	16
Striped hose, all sizes	19
*Striped inverted top for hose, all sizes	76
*Tam o' Shanters, 3 sizes	73
Top ribbing inverted for ½ hose, all sizes	11
*Transferring designs from rows to rounds	59
*Uhlan caps	76
Varieties of horseshoe heel, all sizes	14
Vests, 4 sorts, each in 10 sizes	34
Ditto, No. 1, scale of 10 sizes	90
Ditto, No. 2, scale of 10 sizes	91
Ditto, No. 3, scale of 10 sizes	92
Ditto, No. 4, scale of 10 sizes	93
*Watchguards	51
Welts	8
*Welted comforters, all sizes	45
Welted hose, all sizes	19
*Wrists of babies' gloves, 2 sorts, all sizes	81
Yarns	4

KNITTING FOR EVERYONE.

No. 1.

The need of a seventh edition of this book so soon after the previous one seems to prove the accuracy and efficiency of my principle of having but one set of directions for an article accompanied by a scale of several sizes. The addition of a scale greatly increases the difficulty of writing plain instructions, and the more sizes there are in it the less easy it is to graduate it correctly. All the things in this book, with the exception of some of the larger socks and stockings, have been worked by my hands, in all their different materials, patterns, sizes and sorts, representing a very large number of articles, I therefore know that my directions for making them are correct and hope they may be acceptable to all knitters and induce others to learn and to practice an art so simple, useful and inexpensive.

The dictionary says to knit means to make a texture with one thread or yarn, without a loom or frame, but by means of two or more needles; the word is derived from the Anglo-Saxon cnyttan. The work consists of but one stitch, namely, a loop drawn through another one; the purled stitch is the same as the knitted one in effect, as may be seen in ribs and welts, but is formed backwards, and places the back of the stitch towards the worker; a succession of rows or rounds of these loops produces a piece of knitting. The many beautiful designs in existence useful for numerous purposes, are formed by different arrangements of knitted and purled stitches, by slipping some, by casting on and casting off, by knitting or purling two or more stitches together, and by making new ones.

Scotland and Spain both claim the honour of discovering this art, but Beckmann states that it was invented early in the 16th century in Saxony, by a lady of St. Annaberg, named Barbara, the wife of Christopher Uttmann. It went through Brussels into France, a guild of stocking knitters being established in Paris in 1527, who made St. Fiacre of Scotland their patron saint; thence it soon crossed to England, the first pair of knitted woollen stockings being made by a London apprentice named William Rider, in 1564, and before the end of the century it seems that knitting was generally practised throughout our country. The *advantages of knitting* are many: it is easily learned and carried on; it is most useful, for numerous necessary articles can be knitted; it is inexpensive, the implements being simple and few, and the principal yarns, namely, cotton and wool, costing but little; it can be done when one is feeling too weak or too tired for other work, or even when lying down, or in the twilight, or when travelling, or in many odd moments which would otherwise be wasted, or when conversation or reading is going on, some women even knitting and reading aloud at the same time; and lastly, knitted things are warmer, wear longer, and wash much better than woven ones, also the parts liable to wear out more quickly than the rest can be strengthened by using double material, and can easily be renewed when necessary. This useful art has lately been revived by the most sensible decree of fashion and the educational authorities, and my hope is that my books and scales may promote its extension.

Knitting may be generally divided into two parts; Plain, which is the most useful, and what is usually called Fancy, which also is often applied to necessary as well as to ornamental household things. The former is of two sorts: *garter knitting*, which is worked in rows, both sides being alike and rough; and *stocking knitting*, which is worked in rows or rounds, both sides being different, one rough and the other smooth, to produce the latter in rows every other row must be purled. The many beautiful things suggested by the term Fancy knitting include circles, edgings, squares, insertions, repeating designs, etc., these last are so called for lack of one word containing the idea of the repetition of the pattern both in the width and in the length; they have a certain number of stitches and rows in a pattern and can be extended both ways. Those in my books are very varied in their appearance, their size with regard to the number of stitches and rows and their suitability for a very large variety of different purposes. They and the insertion are of two sorts, close and open; the close ones have no made stitches and are suitable for bath towels, toilet covers, etc.; the open ones abound in made stitches and are suitable for curtains, shawls, etc.; the marginal stitches in articles made with these last designs must be knitted rather loosely, as the made stitches cause the rest of the work to expand. Those with the back rows plain can be worked most quickly, and many of those can be used equally well for rows or rounds. Most of them too will be easier to work and to remember if their construction be observed: some have a middle stitch, the rest being arranged alike on each side; others maintain the same number of stitches in each pattern row or round; and in others again the number of stitches is increased or reduced as the pattern progresses and at the end of it the original number is restored. For comforters, curtains, shawls, etc., both sides of which should be alike, the plain back rows had better be knitted instead of purled, therefore choose a design or insertion the beauty of which depends more upon its outline than its surface. The following designs I have for many years found to be the most admired and the most generally applicable to all sorts of articles: close, Huckaback 2, Roma 1; open, Hemstitch 2, *Lois; as they are also very easy to work and to remember, they are, with a few others, generally placed first in the directions. Those designs, etc., marked thus, * are in book 2.

Needles and pins should have rather long points, but not too sharp, the best in quality are the easiest to use. Needles are made in three lengths, about 5, 7 and 9 inches; the short ones are useful for making small articles in fine yarn, such as gloves, babies' boots, etc.; the long ones are for stockings, night caps, etc.; their sizes range from 10 to 20. Pins vary in length from 7 to 18 inches; bone and vulcanite ones are smoother than most wooden ones; it is well to use light coloured pins with dark yarns, and vice-versâ; also the larger sizes are best made in vulcanite or wood, these substances being not so heavy as bone or steel; their sizes range from 1 to 12. The sizes of all of them are determined by "The Warleigh knitting gauge," made by Wynn Timmins & Co., Century Works, Commercial Street, Birmingham, from whom it can be had post free for 1s. 6d. Its sizes correspond with those of the trade gauge by which all wire is made, therefore it is correct; as it weighs under half an ounce, it can be kept in a purse or pocket book, and being made of steel it is reliable, for the holes will not enlarge with proper use as is the case with soft metal gauges; also it has the advantage of showing unmistakably the size of a needle, as there is but one place where it will fit, and not two as is frequently seen. Loose knitters should use needles and pins one size smaller than those named in the directions. Persons who knit a large variety of things will find a baize case for the needles almost a necessity, made to roll up and tie, the compartments being numbered for the different sizes; a box also for the pins will be very useful, in which to keep their heads and points intact. A crochet needle is useful for taking up dropped stitches, and an expanding skein winder is a great help to a busy knitter.

The *yarns* needed for my books are the following made by Messrs. Strutt of Belper; correct size and full weight are guaranteed; also the Nos. of the sizes in the knitting cotton, the Angola, the School cotton and the crochet cotton correspond as nearly as can be: best knitting cotton, 3 threads, white, unbleached and coloured, Nos 4 to 16; summer Merino, 3 threads, white and coloured, Nos. 8 to 16, this is a mixture of cotton and wool and is generally called Angola; School knitting cotton, 3 threads, Nos. 4 and 6, this is made in several bright colours very attractive to children; Scouring cotton, 6 threads, unbleached, for floor cloths, etc.; Crochet cotton, white, Nos. 14 to 30; to these must be added all the other wools, etc., named in the following classes. Yarn means spun wool or cotton; these two materials are the ones most generally used in knitting, to them may be added hair, linen and silk. From all these materials a very large variety of beautiful yarns is now made in every possible combination and in all colours, shades and mixtures. Bright colours, such as blue and red, do not wash and wear so well as brown, drab or grey in their different shades; scarlet is apt to dazzle the eyes. The undyed or sanitary wool is the best to wear next to the skin, it is made in several sizes and shades so as to suit all tastes and purposes, and is nearly as soft as that queen of wools Lady Betty, so called after the wife of the poet Young. Experience alone can decide which will wear best; I name those only that are well known and which may be called standard ones, being distinct sorts, the same in all respects, or very nearly so, for years past, by whom ever made; they will, I think, form a sufficiently large selection from which to choose for most ordinary purposes, several of them being made in two or more sizes. To those however, who have used other sorts, or wish to do so, the following *classification of yarns* according to size will be a help in choosing substitutes. Any other yarn, instead of the one named, can be used for an article with the needles that are directed for it, if it be of the same sort, size and quality, so as to make the article of the same durability and size; perfect exactness may not be attainable between the two, but by drawing them both at the same time through the fingers it will soon be felt if they sufficiently match. If a thicker article is needed than any for which I give directions, choose the yarn from the next class coarser and use needles one size larger, then work from the scale one or two sizes smaller; but to produce the same effect with different needles and yarns is the result of much experience. Though all the yarns in a class are not exactly the same size, a thing it would be difficult if not impossible to accomplish with such widely differing materials, yet they are as nearly so as my experience and knowledge of existing yarns could arrange and graduate, consistently with including those most generally used and avoiding too many classes. Almost invariably in the directions in my books the succeeding sizes of needles are used with the succeeding classes of yarns. Class I. Cotton 4, 5 ply Fingering, 4 ply Fleecy, double Berlin, Alloa. Class II. Cotton 6,

4 ply Fingering, 3 ply Fleecy, 5 ply Berlin Fingering. Class III. Cotton and Angola 8, 3 ply Fingering, 2 ply Fleecy, 4 ply Berlin Fingering, 4 ply Lady Betty, single Berlin, Welsh yarn. Class IV. Cotton and Angola 10, 2 ply Fingering, 3 ply Berlin Fingering, 3 ply Lady Betty, Andalusian. Class V. Cotton and Angola 12, 2 ply Lady Betty, Shetland, Filoselle. Class VI. Cotton and Angola and Crochet Cotton 14, Pyrenees, smooth spun Silk. Class VII. Cotton and Angola and Crochet Cotton 16. All wools should be wound just before being used, and as loosely as possible, particularly the better and softer sorts and qualities; to accomplish this lay the thumb lightly on the ball and wind the wool over it, drawing it out occasionally. Short pieces of yarn can be used for Cuffs, Doll's things, Laundry bags, etc., and the ends that are too short to be knitted up can be kept in a bag to fill balls and cushions.

The following *appropriation of yarns* may be useful. For women's and girls' stockings for ordinary winter wear, use 4 ply Fingering, for finer and softer ones, 3 ply Fingering or Andalusian; for ordinary summer wear, Angola and Cotton 10, for finer and best ones, Silk. For men's and boys' hose for coldest weather and roughest wear, such as boating, cycling, shooting, etc., use Alloa, which is very strong, or 5 ply Fingering, which is softer, or unbleached Cotton 6, which is stronger and warmer than white cotton and than most Angola; for ordinary wear, Welsh yarn, or 4 ply Fingering, or Angola and Cotton 10; for best evening ones, Silk. For little children's socks use Andalusian or Angola and Cotton 12, 14 and 16, Filoselle for winter, Silk for summer. For babies to wear next to the skin nothing is softer than Lady Betty wool, 2, 3 or 4 thread, according to the time of year; or Silk which is soft, strong and warm.

The following *selection of needles, pins, and yarns* may be a guide to beginners. For bread, cheese, fish and tray doileys, needles 14, knitting cotton 12; or needles 15, cotton 14, crochet cotton 18; or needles 16, crochet cotton 22. For dessert doileys, needles 18, linen 30. For fruit and biscuit dishes, needles 18, crochet cotton 30. For pin-cushion covers and toilet doileys, needles 16, crochet cotton

22; or needles 17, crochet cotton 26. For splash curtains and window blinds, needles 8, cotton 12; or needles 9, cotton 14; or needles 14, crochet cotton 14. For antimacassars, pins 6, cotton 4; or pins 7, cotton 6; or pins 8, cotton 12; or pins 9, cotton 14; or needles 14, crochet cotton 18. For window curtains, needles 5, cotton 8; or needles 6, cotton 10. For counterpanes, cradle quilts and toilet covers, needles 13, cotton 8; or needles 14, cotton 10. For comb bags and night dress cases, needles 14, cotton 12; or needles 15, cotton 14, these should be lined with Turkey twill or coloured cambric. For shawls, wraps, clouds and scarves, pins 7, Shetland; or pins 6, Andalusian, 2 ply Fingering, 3 ply Lady Betty; or pins 5, single Berlin, 3 ply Fingering, 4 ply Lady Betty. For veils, pins 8, Shetland; or pins 9, Pyrenees. Suitable needles, pins and yarns for other things will be found under their different headings. Two sorts and sizes of yarn in one article sometimes look well, and two colours or shades well contrasted or blended form a pleasing variety.

Stitches can be made in three ways: by knitting into the back as well as into the front of a stitch, this is best for plain and close work; by knitting under the yarn just below and between two stitches, this makes a small hole and is called knitting up or raising a stitch, it is seldom used as it drags the yarn above its level; and by crossing the yarn over the needle, this makes a large hole. In all my books the last way is to be used unless otherwise directed; to make two or more stitches in this way put the yarn two or more times round the needle and in this case the second and all alternate stitches must be purled in the following row, taking care that they do not slip off the needle before this is accomplished; to make a stitch after knitting and before purling, the yarn must be put in front of the needle and then wound entirely round it; to make one after purling and before knitting, the yarn need only be left in front of the needle, in both cases make sure that it crosses the needle.

Ridges are made by knitting plain in rows, two rows making one ridge; they produce what is called garter knitting and contract the work in its length. *Ribs* are perpendicular, being made the same way as the work; they can be produced in rows or in rounds by alternately knitting and purling one stitch or more; to rib in any number, say 3, a multiple of twice that number, in this case 6, must be cast on, 12, 18 etc.; this is imperative in ribbing in rounds. *Welts* are horizontal, being made across the work; they can be produced in rows by alternately knitting and purling any even number of rows and then by alternately purling and knitting the same or any other even number of rows, so that two knitted rows or two purled ones will be next to each other, thus making welts on each side of the work; alternately knit and purl any number in rounds. Begin both ribs and welts with knitting both in rows and in rounds; both sides of the work in all three cases are alike.

The only accurate, and therefore the most satisfactory way of marking the size of an article, especially a complex one, is by the number of stitches and of rows or rounds in its different parts; thus it will be found very convenient to work by a scale, and to mark the number of plain rows and rounds in tens, and the increasings and reducings, four stitches from the end of the row or round, with a small wool needle and fine cotton of a contrasting colour, unless when making white things, used double to prevent losing the needle. This *stitch and row metre* is very simple and its use should be taught with the knitting; put a long stitch at the hundredth row or round and at the beginning of the different parts of an article, such as the flap of a heel or the finger of a glove, so that a glance will show the place and thus save much time often spent in counting. The size of an article depends on four things: the number of stitches cast on and of rows or rounds worked, the size of the needles or pins, the sort of yarn used, and the worker: therefore though the first three conditions can be ensured, yet as knitters vary so much in their work, the first thing made must almost necessarily be an experiment to a small extent with regard to size, though not to shape if the directions are correctly followed. In things where the fit is important it is well to begin with a small size, so as not to expend much time and labour and meet with disappointment; No. 3 is advisable, as its figures are in the directions, which may make a first attempt easier to some persons.

Beginners may find it well to work in the following succession: Slate rubbers, Knee caps, Mittens before Mufflers and Gloves, then a small pair of Socks before Stockings; this last is most important for children, as they may be discouraged, or may even dislike the work by having to do a long leg before beginning the interesting part of the heel; also the time for useful work in schools is so short that it should be put to the best advantage by letting a child go through all the parts of a sock, which are the same as those of a stocking, four or five times before leaving school to fix them in the memory. The *hyphens* mark certain divisions in the pattern, or precede or follow a part of the pattern that is the same in every row; they will be found a help to the memory. *Abbreviations*, especially arbitrary ones, being generally disliked, I have used only these; R. H. N. and L. H. N. for right and left hand needle; *over*, which means put the slipped stitch over the knitted one which immediately follows it, or over the two knitted together; this way of reducing is necessary *before* the middle of many designs to match the reducing *after* it. In all my books there is only one mode of expressing an action, and that a simple one, as a varied and complicated phraseology, such as is often met with, is very puzzling to anyone, particularly to a novice in the art. It will be well to read the directions before working from them. When directions are given for two or more sizes of an article, care must be taken to use the right figures throughout, according to the size that is being worked. In sewing seams, especially those in articles worn next to the skin, draw the edges together so as to avoid a ridge, in this way they may be made so flat as scarcely to be felt; some of them can be crocheted instead of sewn, this takes more yarn but looks neater. A very large variety of useful things can be made by a little thought and by a judicious combination of the Repeating designs, Insertions, etc., in all the books; this will be found an interesting occupation and may be made very profitable also, as articles well made by hand are in constant demand. The following will be found easy work for invalids or for those whose sight is not good; Antimacassars in cotton 4 or 6, Bath towels and squares, Comforters, Cuffs, Hoods, Knee caps, and Vests. I have worked all the Edgings, Insertions and Repeating designs in all my books three or four times while taking them through the press, after they were in print, the figures may therefore be relied upon for accuracy; I have also tried to make the books suggestive as well as instructive. Children should be taught to knit as a reward for doing plain needle work well, this will tend to make a pleasure of both employments. Boys should be encouraged to learn and to continue knitting, this is done in some schools; they as well as the girls should learn the Maxims for knitters, where it is possible the reason for the maxim is given to make it more interesting and more easy to remember; they should also be taught to knit neither too tightly nor too loosely; in the former case the wool mills when washed and becomes hard, in the latter case the article does not keep its shape well when washed; the stitches should just move readily along the needle. My scales are for persons of the usual proportions, individual variations can easily be suited by adding to the number of the rows or rounds in the different parts or by taking from them. This book has been adopted by the London School Board for many years and is on their requisition list; it is also used in several Training Colleges and in a very large and rapidly increasing number of Schools, Industrial Institutions and working Guilds, etc. It is some years since I first published my Directions and Scales for Socks and Stockings, lately they have been republished twice, under another name, the directions are altered but the scale left as I made it, this leads me to state that the principle and the carrying of it out in every particular are my idea, experience has proved that my plan is the right one. I shall be glad if persons will no more print any of my directions and scales without my leave.

SOCKS AND STOCKINGS.

Four needles 12, 5 ply Fingering, Alloa ; or needles 13, 4 ply Fingering, Cotton 6 ; or needles 14, 3 ply Fingering, Welsh yarn, Angola and Cotton 8 ; or needles 15, 2 ply Fingering, Andalusian, Angola and Cotton 10 ; or needles 16, Filoselle, Angola and Cotton 12; or needles 17, Silk, Angola and Cotton 14.

The figures refer to No. 3 long sock of the scale.

Cast 22 stitches on to each of the first two needles and 23 on to the third, making a *total* of 67.

For the top rib 38 rounds in ones, twos or fours ; sizes 1, 4, 7 and 10 in socks and stockings can be ribbed here in threes ; long socks or ¾ hose must be ribbed here in ones. Begin every round with knitting, the odd stitch at the end of the third or last needle is to be alternately knitted and purled, or is to be purled in every round, which is more quickly done ; it will form the seam in the leg and will be the last stitch in every round ; in the long socks this stitch must be omitted when casting on, and added when the top ribbing is ended by knitting into the back and then into the front of the last stitch in the first plain round. This ribbing prevents the top from rolling up. It is well to put this *top ribbing upside down* when making large socks in a fine and expensive yarn, particularly if they are likely to be dyed, as is often done with silk ones for evening wear, which have been made in the colours of a College, School or Club, etc. Ribbing will not unravel well backwards as plain knitting will do, yet the first inch or more is apt to get very much stretched, rendering the sock almost useless by falling down ; to obviate this, cast off loosely when the top ribbing is ended, knit up the same number of stitches from the casting on round, and continue as before directed. This will be a saving of yarn as well as of time, for the same yarn can generally be used again, there being little or no wear at that part of the sock. *A hem with a notched edge* can be made for stockings instead of ribbing, work thus : after casting on, knit twelve rounds plain, make one and knit two together all round, knit twelve rounds plain, fold it to make a hem and knit the round on the needles with the first or casting on round; or, cast all the stitches on to one needle, alternately knit and purl eight rows, divide the stitches on to three needles according to the scale, make the circle and knit four rounds, make one and knit two together all round, knit twelve rounds plain, fold it to make a hem and knit the round on the needles with the first or casting on round : in either case the width of the hem can be varied according to the size of the stocking and the sort of yarn used. When knitting stockings for a family, it will be convenient for each person to choose a colour, and to have two or three rounds of that colour knitted into the ribbing, or inside the hem, or just below either, that it may be seen at a glance to whom the stocking belongs; the socks can have a few stitches of the colour put into the sole in the shape of a diamond or otherwise. Knit 36 *plain leg rounds*, but in the sixth of them after the third stitch, make one and knit two together, or purl alternate stitches beginning with the fourth; do either 3 times to mark the *size*. Any letters or figures can be worked under the mark for the size, or in the sole, by purling the stitches according to a sampler.

The calf of the leg is worked thus : in the next round after the plain ones, knit one, knit two together, knit to within four stitches of the end of the round, slip one, knit one, put the slipped stitch over the knitted one, knit one, purl the seam stitch; in fine material two stitches can be left between the seam and each reduction; when using a Repeating design, close or open, leave no stitches between them. There are to be 3 of these *leg reducing rounds*, with five plain ones after each except the last, so making every sixth round a reducing one; there will be 13 *rounds in the calf*, including the first and last reducing rounds. In stockings and large socks it will be well here occasionally to equalise the number of stitches on the needles by putting two at a time from each end of the middle or second needle on to each side needle. For a very tall person it may be necessary to knit six or seven plain rounds after every reducing one, as well as add to the plain rounds before and after the calf. The *number of stitches* now on the needles will be 61 ; six fewer than the number that was cast on, because there are, in this size, 3 pairs of reducings, generally called, 3 leg reductions. Knit 18 *plain ankle rounds*. In the stockings there are as many plain rounds here as there are stitches on the needles, omitting the seam.

Divide for the heel thus : halve the stitches, put 31, that is a quarter on each side of the seam stitch, on to one needle for the *heel*; the rest, namely 30, which are for the *instep*, divide equally on to two needles. If it be needed to strengthen the heel, add some much finer yarn here, for if the heel be too thick it breaks away from the leg; Shetland or Pyrenees wool, 2 ply Fingering, Saxony or Angola mending on cards, are all suitable; a little care is needed here to prevent dividing the two threads and dropping one.

Work the heel flap thus : alternately purl and knit the heel stitches in rows till there are four rows fewer than the number in the scale, preserving the seam by knitting the middle stitch in the purled or back rows. The first of these rows will be a purled one, the last of them will be a knitted one. Purl a row; in the next row knit to within three stitches of the seam, slip one, knit one, put the slipped stitch over the knitted one, knit one, purl the seam stitch, knit one, knit two together, knit to the end; purl a row; knit another reducing row as before, leaving two stitches between the seam and each reduction. These two pairs of reducings in the flap round it a little, and so make it fit better, also they make the number of *rows in the heel flap* 24. Purl a row.

Turn the heel thus: knit to the third stitch inclusive beyond the seam, knit the next two together, turn and purl to the third stitch inclusive beyond the seam, purl the next two together, turn again and work backwards and forwards in rows, keeping only the 9 *middle stitches* in every row, knitting in or purling in, with the last of the middle stitches, one of those left at the sides till all are taken in; continue the seam as in the flap. The first of these rows will be a knitted one, the last of them will be a purled one. Knit the middle stitches, in this row discontinue the seam, and at the end of it cut off the added yarn. This is called the Horseshoe or Dutch heel; it is the one most generally used, being the best shape, easy to make and to darn and very comfortable to wear. A variation of it can be made thus : knit to within two stitches of the seam, slip one, knit one, put the slipped stitch over the knitted one, purl the seam stitch, knit two together, finish knitting the 9 middle stitches, then knit the first of those left at the side, turn and purl the 9 middle stitches, then purl the first of those left at the side, turn again and work backwards and forwards in rows, keeping only the 9 middle stitches in every row, making two reducings in every knitted or front row, and knitting or purling at the end of every row one of those left at the sides till all are taken in. Another variation can be made in the larger sizes, by knitting from one to four stitches between the seam and each reducing. *The heel can be made loose* thus : divide for it ten rounds before the usual place, also begin the extra yarn here; alternately purl and knit the heel stitches for ten rows, then continue according to the scale as before directed; when the flap is turned cast off the middle stitches instead of knitting them, leaving an end about ten inches long; then alternately purl and knit the instep stitches for ten rows, the first of them will be a purled one, leave an end of yarn at the beginning of them; in the last of these rows, which will be a knitted one, put the last five stitches on to another needle, on to this other needle cast the right number of side stitches according to the scale, also cast on to it half the number of the heel middle stitches and one more, which one more will meet the seam stitch in the cast off heel and will be the last stitch in the round : purl this last stitch in the first six rounds, this will make it easier when sewing up the heel to prevent puckering or stretching one side ; on to a third needle cast the rest of the heel middle stitches and the other side stitches; with a fourth needle knit the first five instep stitches and put them on to the third needle, so making a circle : thus, half the heel middle stitches, all one side stitches and five of the instep stitches will be on each side needle and the rest of the instep stitches will be on the second or middle needle. Finish the round, that is, work to the seam stitch in the heel, knit two rounds plain then continue according to the scale as before directed, making the ankle and heel reducings in the usual way and places. Sew up the heel making the two seams under it meet. The great advantage of working the heel thus is that it can be replaced when worn out, with very little trouble and with no waste of yarn, as the instep and sole will last out three or four heels, and can be left untouched till the whole foot needs to be cut off.

Work the ankle gussets thus: with the needle on which are the heel stitches knit up 14 *side stitches*, into the inside loops, down the first side of the heel flap and knit off five of the instep stitches; with a second needle knit the rest of the instep stitches except the last five; with a third needle knit these five and knit up 14 stitches, into the inside loops, down the other side of the heel flap; with a fourth needle knit half the heel stitches, including the seam stitch, and put them on to the third needle, that is, the one just filled. The seam stitch will continue to be the last in the round, but it must not be purled. Half the heel middle stitches, all one side stitches and five of the instep stitches will be on each side needle, that is, on the first and on the third, and the rest of the instep stitches will be on the second or middle needle. If the heel is strengthened as directed above, be careful not to divide the two threads in knitting up the side stitches; also it will be well to knit up one, two or three extra stitches on each side, according to the size of the sock, as the added yarn lengthens the heel flap a little, and in consequence there must be one, two or three more pairs of ankle reducings, to make the right number of stitches in the foot according to the scale, these extra rounds can be deducted from the number of plain ones in the foot, if it be thought too long. The *number of stitches* now on the needles will be 67. Knit two rounds plain, the first and last instep stitches, each of which is the fifth stitch from the instep end of each side needle, are to be alternately knitted and purled, or to be purled in every round, which is more quickly done, they will form the side seams in the foot, and will not be needed in ribbed socks and stockings. In the next round on the first needle knit two, knit two together, knit to within seven stitches of the end, slip one, knit one, put the slipped stitch over the knitted one, these being the last two of the first side stitches, purl one, knit four; on the second needle knit the instep stitches, there will be ten fewer than their whole number; on the third needle knit four, purl one, knit two together, these being the first two of the other side stitches, knit to within four stitches of the end, slip one, knit one, put the slipped stitch over the knitted one, knit two. Repeat these reducing rounds making 1 pair of *heel* and 2 pairs of *ankle reducings* with two plain rounds after each reducing round except the last one. The *number of stitches* now on the needles will be 61, the same as before dividing for the heel. Knit 44 *plain foot rounds*. For a very long foot add to these plain rounds.

Divide for the toe thus: halve the stitches, keep a quarter of the number on each side needle and put the rest on to the second or middle needle; there will be 30 stitches under the foot and 31 above it. The stitches can be knitted into this arrangement in the last plain round in the foot. Here discontinue the side seams. If it be needed to strengthen the toe add some finer yarn here. In the next round on the first needle knit to within four stitches of the end, knit two together, knit two; on the second needle knit two, knit two together, knit to within four stitches of the end, knit two together, knit two; on the third needle knit two, knit two together, knit to the end. This will make a reducing at each end of each side of the toe, and will lessen the number of stitches by four in every reducing round. There are to be 11 of these *toe reducing rounds*, with three plain ones after the first, two after the second, and one after each of the others, finish with a plain round. The *number of stitches* now on the needles will be 17. *Cast off the toe* thus: knit to the end of the first needle, this will bring the yarn to the side of the toe; put the stitches that are on the side needles on to one, these are the sole stitches, with a third needle cast off double by knitting a stitch on the instep needle and one on the sole needle together, knit another pair together, then put the first on the R.H.N. over the second, knit another pair together and continue as before till all are cast off; in doing this three stitches must be knitted together in the middle of the row, as one side will have one more stitch than the other side; also knit the first four stitches together and the last four together to make the toe less square. This is called the manufacturer's toe; its very general use proves it is a favourite one.

The instep and sole can be divided, work thus: when the heel is turned do not knit the middle stitches nor cast them off, but cut off the yarn; put all the instep stitches on to one needle; then knit up the side stitches, the work must be held with the outside of it towards the knitter, knit half the heel middle stitches, including the seam stitch on to this needle; with another needle knit the rest of the middle stitches and knit up the other side stitches. Alternately purl and knit all these stitches in rows, not working the instep stitches, begin with a purled row; make the right number of heel and ankle reducings in the usual places, according to the scale, but two stitches from each end of the row; knit or purl two together according to the position of the reductions, that is, whether they occur in a knitted front row or in a purled back one; then knit the same number of plain rows as there are plain rounds in the scale, leave these sole stitches on one needle or put them on to a piece of coarse cotton; cut off the yarn, leaving an end to sew up one side of the foot. With the instep stitches alternately purl and knit the same number of plain rows as there are plain rounds in the scale, and as many more rows as there are rounds in the ankle gusset, namely from knitting up the side stitches to the last ankle reducing inclusive; there will be three times as many extra rows as there are pairs of ankle reductions; this will make the instep as long as the sole.

If the sock is being ribbed, the ribs must be preserved in the back rows of the instep by knitting the stitches that were purled in the front rows and by purling the rest; if it is striped as well, knit all the stitches in the first row of every stripe if it is a front row and purl them all if it is a back row, this will prevent the half stitches of the added colour shewing on the outside of the sock; for doing this there had better be an even number of rows in every stripe, that each may begin on one and the same side of the instep and thus avoid having constantly to cut off the yarn. The last of these instep rows will be a knitted or front one. Make the circle by knitting the sole stitches, knit one round plain and finish the toe as before directed; sew up the seams and darn in all the ends. The advantage of this divided foot is that time and yarn are saved, for the heel, sole and toe can be renewed without undoing the instep; also the stripes can be put in the instep only and not in the sole, which is better for darning.

If *ribbed socks or stockings* be needed, work thus: omit the seam stitch when casting on, and work the hem or rib the right number for the top in ones or twos; then rib in ones throughout; or, knit 3 and purl 1 throughout; sizes 1, 4, 7 and 10 can be ribbed in knit 2 and purl 1; or, the large sizes in knit 4 and purl 2, for this put a multiple of 3, 4 or 6 on to each needle; or, alternately rib in ones or twos for 3 or 4 rounds and knit plain for 2 or 3 rounds; in any case mark the size in the middle of the hem, on either side, or in the sole. Continue the ribbing a little way down the heel, leaving off in a short point; to do this work thus: in every fourth or sixth row omit both outer purled stitches, that is, knit them and continue knitting them; repeat this till only the seam stitch is left to be purled. In the instep rib up to the toe reductions; the ribs here also can be left off in a short point. All else is to be worked as before directed, except that in the calf, leave no stitches between the reductions and the seam. The knees of children's stockings had better be knitted plain, being easier to darn; they can be strengthened in the same way as the heels. These are sometimes called *rig and fur hose*, these two words being North country dialect for the ridge and furrow of a newly ploughed field, to which a ribbed stocking has some resemblance.

If *welted socks or stockings* be needed, work thus: for the small sizes, knit 3 or 4 rounds plain then purl 1 or 2 rounds; for the large sizes, knit 4 or 5 rounds plain then purl 2 or 3 rounds; in either case continue the welts half-way down the heel flap and in the instep, but not the sole, up to the toe reductions; all else is to be worked as before directed. The welts should always be narrower than the space that divides them.

If *striped socks or stockings* be needed, work thus; begin the second colour after the top ribbing or the hem is finished, change the colour at the first stitch in the round, do not cut off the yarn each time but purl the seam stitch with both colours and carry on the yarn not in use to the next stripe, inside the leg; take care not to pull the yarn from the last stripe, but keep the work flat; the width of the stripes and the arrangement of the colours must be according to taste, but for large socks and for stockings it will be convenient for counting the rounds if the stripes are 10 rounds wide, or if 2 or 3 stripes occupy 10 rounds.

If *fancy work socks or stockings* be needed, use a close or open repeating design, such as Huckaback 2, Roma, *Emerald, Hemstitch, *Heene, Willow-leaf, *Colonia, *Gratia, or *Irene; see contents in each book. It is well to work a small piece of the selected design before beginning the hose, as a little counting of the stitches may be needed to arrange it correctly.

No. 1 stocking and No. 2 sock and long sock are the same size, as may be seen by referring to the scale, beginning with the stitches after the calf. A short stocking is for gartering below the knee, a long one should well cover it, for the latter add to the plain rounds before the calf. It is well to begin both hose of a pair at the same time, so as to fix all the parts in the memory and to prevent the second one being so superior to the first one as to spoil the pair; it is convenient also to work the difficult parts, such as the heel and toe, during a quiet time, and to reserve the plain parts, such as the leg and foot, for reading and talking hours. The words in the scale, also the different parts of a sock or stocking are put in italics in the directions, to make it easier to refer to the scale, or to any part of a sock to see how it is worked.

THE WARLEIGH MUSICAL DRILL.

Little children should learn to knit with short needles 11 or 12, the points being not sharp enough to prick them, yet not too blunt to go easily into the stitches, and with unbleached cotton 4, 6, or 8; or School cotton 4 or 6; or good, soft string; these being less apt to split than wool. They should be taught the rudiments of the art in the following order: the knitting stitch, the purling stitch, casting on, casting off; these four things should be kept distinct, and each should be thoroughly practised and well known before beginning the next; they should also have a piece of knitting to begin upon, not too wide for a small hand to hold, and long enough to hang down below the fingers but without resting in the lap, this is to prevent the work twisting round the needle which is apt to occur in baby hands, 10 to 14 stitches wide and 4 to 6 inches long will answer well; the discarded remnants of the Standard above them will suit the purpose, 3 or 4 rows being knitted by the teacher, or by an elder girl, as a correct foundation. Attention to these few small but important things will greatly facilitate the lesson.

The placing of the needles and cotton in the hands varies even in the English way of knitting, for which only, this drill and these remarks are intended. The difference consists chiefly in the position of the R.H.N., some persons placing it above the hand, resting it on the junction of the thumb and forefinger, others placing it below, the latter way perhaps had its origin in the use of the sheath, fixed in the waist at the right side, seldom seen now and quite unnecessary; the first way is the most usual, the L. N. being under the hand. For making both the knitting stitch and the purling stitch the cotton should be held by the R.H. thus: over the little finger, under the next two, and over the forefinger; it should be thrown by the tip of the forefinger round the point of the R.H.N., the right thumb should not move from its needle, still less should the R.H. leave its needle to the chance of falling out of the stitches that are upon it, while it is throwing the cotton round the point. Both stitches are produced by four actions, the words in italics shew the only difference between them.

KNITTING DRILL. 1st. Put the R.H.N. *before* the cotton, pointing *from* you, *down* into the stitch that is on the L.H.N. 2nd. Place the cotton under and round in front of the R.H.N., and *put* it back over it. 3rd. *Draw* this cotton *to* you, through the stitch, by means of the R.H.N., so making a new stitch. 4th. Slip the stitch off the L.H.N., it will fall below and *backwards*, and the new one rising out of it will be on the R.H.N.

PURLING DRILL. 1st. Put the R.H.N. *behind* the cotton, pointing *to* you, *up* into the stitch that is on the L.H.N. 2nd. Place the cotton back over the R.H.N., and *bring* it under and round in front of it. 3rd. *Push* this cotton *from* you, through the stitch, by means of the R.H.N., so making a new stitch. 4th. Slip the stitch off the L.H.N., it will fall below and *forwards*, and the new one rising out of it will be on the R.H.N.

For both knitting and purling this can be reduced thus: Put the needle in. Place the cotton round. Bring this cotton through. Slip the old stitch off. When both stitches can readily be made, this also can be shortened, the first and last words only in each sentence being used: Put in. Place round. Bring through. Slip off. To which echo answers, when perfection is attained: In. Round. Through. Off. The preceding air was composed for this drill and its two abbreviations to make the knitting lesson attractive to children, and was harmonized to make it more interesting for teachers who are musical.

CASTING ON. Make a loop by drawing the yarn through a single twist that has already been made near to its end, put this loop on to the L.H.N., * knit into this stitch and put the new one so made on to the L.H.N. but without taking the R.H.N. out of it, repeat from * till the right number is obtained; this should be done loosely.

CASTING OFF. 1st. Knit the first two stitches, * put the first over the second, leaving one only on the R.H.N., knit another, repeat from * till all are off the L.H.N., draw the yarn through the last stitch; this should be done loosely. 2nd. Knit two together, * return this stitch to the L.H.N., knit the next one with it, repeat from * till all are off the L.H.N., draw the yarn through the last stitch.

MAXIMS FOR KNITTERS.

1. Needles have a point at each end, pins have a point at one end and a head at the other. 2. Rows are worked backwards and forwards with two needles or pins, rounds are worked in a circle with four or more needles. 3. Do not mis-apply the words needle, pin, row, round, ridge, rib, and welt by interchanging them. 4. Cast on and cast off loosely, particularly when ribbing, so that the edges of an article can be stretched nearly as much as the rest of it. 5. Leave out an end of the yarn to shew where the row or round begins. 6. Darn in all the ends with a wool needle when the work is finished, leaving an inch over, inside round, work to

prevent their working through to the outer side. 7. When knitting in rows slip the first stitch the knitting way, unless a chain edge is needed, for which slip it the purling way. 8. A front row is one which is being worked while the right side of the article or the design is facing the knitter. 9. Do not break off the yarn, but cut it. 10. When knitting in rounds work the first two stitches and the last two on each needle rather tightly, to prevent the appearance of a Jacob's ladder. 11. When the colour of the yarn is changed in any case the first row or round must be knitted plain on the right side of the work, to prevent the half stitches shewing outside. 12. To join the yarn reverse its ends so as to have four inches double, work six stitches with them so, keeping both ends inside round work and at the back of flat work. 13. Count the stitches occasionally in plain rows and rounds, to see that the number is right, and that no stitches are made and none dropped. 14. When a needle has all its stitches on, put them into the middle of it, to prevent their falling off at either end. 15. Coarse cotton or fine string of a contrasting colour to the work, should be used for putting through stitches that are to be off the needle for a time. 16. Leave off knitting in the middle of a needleful, the fullest if there be a difference, to lessen the chance of losing a needle, and to allow of work in rounds being folded flat without stretching the corners. 17. Push the needles into the ball without splitting the yarn. 18. If the work is ribbed or in rounds give it a slight pull lengthways before putting it away.

CHAIN EDGE.

This is used for plain knitting in rows, or for plain margins divided by a design; it is prettier than the edge made by slipping the first stitch the knitting way and is also looser, so it should not be used for strips that are to be sewn together, but for comforters, etc. Work thus: slip the first stitch in the row the purling way; to do this put the yarn in front of the R.H.N., slip the stitch off the L.H.N. as if for purling, but without forming a new stitch, put the yarn behind the R.H.N., work the rest of the row.

CODE KNITTING.

Below Standard I.

Two short needles 11, unbleached, or School Cotton 6, or ⅜ oz. of 1 ply Fingering.

For the *Knitting pin Drill* see page 20. For *a strip* cast on 24 stitches, knit plain for 15 inches. Sew together 5 of the cotton strips for a blackboard rubber, or 3 of them 9 inches long for a slate rubber or bath square. The best of the woollen strips can be used for children's petticoats; sew or crochet them together, put them into a band and bind the placket hole and the bottom edge with strong braid.

Standard I.

Two short needles 12, unbleached Cotton 8, or ½ oz. of single Berlin.

The needles and yarn are a size finer here. For *a strip* cast on 26 stitches, knit plain for 15 inches. Sew together the cotton strips as above; or 7 of them 21 inches long or 8 of them 24 inches long for a duster; or 9 or 10 of them 1¼ yard long for a toilet cover; or a larger size will do for a cradle quilt. For the last two purposes they can be worked in a small repeating design, thus: knit 5 ridges plain, then knit the first 5 stitches and the last 5 plain in every row and work the 16 middle ones in Huckaback 2, Roma 1 and 2, or *Irene No. 1, 1 and 2; finish with 5 ridges plain. The needles and cotton used for these strips are the same as those used for bath towels, gloves and squares, blackboard and slate rubbers and dusters.

Comforters.

Two pins 4, 3½ ozs. of 4 ply Fingering; or pins 5, 3¼ ozs. of single Berlin.

For *a comforter* cast on 38 stitches in 4 ply Fingering, or 44 in single Berlin. Knit 2 rows, in the next row knit 1 and make 1 and knit 2 together, repeat to the end; this will make holes for the fringe. Knit 160 ridges in Fingering, or 190 in single Berlin. Work a row of holes as before, knit 2 rows and cast off. For the fringe knot 3 or 4 pieces of the same wool, 10 inches long, into every hole. These will be about 9 inches wide by 1¼ yard long; the Berlin ones, being softer, are for girls, the Fingering ones for boys. The best of these strips can be sewn together as coverlets for cradles, etc.; for this purpose they can be worked in a small repeating design that has 2, 3 or 6 stitches in a pattern, see contents in each book, in this case slip the first stitch and knit the last in every row.

Standard II.
No. 1. *Cuffs* welted in rows.

Two needles 11, 4 ply Fingering; or needles 12, single Berlin.

Cast on 36 stitches in 4 ply Fingering, or 38 in single Berlin. Knit rows 1, 3 and 5, and purl 2, 4 and 6, then purl rows 7, 9 and 11, and knit 8, 10 and 12; this will make welts, 6 rows wide, across the work, and is called welting in sixes. Repeat these 12 rows till there are 12 welts in Fingering and 14 in single Berlin, that is 6 or 7 on each side. Cast off and sew the ends together, or cast off double with the first row. For a smaller size, cast on 28 in Fingering and work 10 welts, 5 on each side; or cast on 30 in single Berlin and work 12 welts, 6 on each side. For a doll, cast on 16 in single Berlin and work 8 welts, 4 rows wide. The welted cuffs are put first because they have whole rows of the knitting stitch and of the purling stitch, which is easier for children than alternately knitting and purling 2 or more stitches as is done in ribbing.

No. 2. *Cuffs* ribbed in rows.

Two needles 12, 4 ply Fingering; or needles 13, single Berlin.

Cast on 48 stitches in 4 ply Fingering, or 52 in single Berlin. Alternately knit 2 and purl 2 throughout every row, beginning each row with knitting; this will make ribs, 2 stitches wide, the same way as the work, and is called ribbing in twos. Rib 50 rows in Fingering, or 52 in single Berlin. Cast off loosely; cut off the wool leaving an end to sew the sides together. For a smaller size, cast on 40 in Fingering and rib 46 rows; or cast on 44 in single Berlin and rib 48 rows. For a doll, cast on 24 in single Berlin and rib 24 rows in ones.

E

Standard III.

No. 1. *Cuffs* welted in rounds.

Four needles 11, 4 ply Fingering; or needles 12, single Berlin.

Cast on for No. 3 in the scale in Fingering, or for No. 4 in single Berlin. As it is difficult to avoid the appearance of a Jacob's ladder when purling in rounds, it will be well to work these cuffs with the wrong side out, the right side being that on which there is a larger number of welts; therefore first knit 6 rounds, then purl 6 rounds. Repeat these 12 rounds till there are 15 welts, that is, 8 outside and 7 inside, in Fingering, or 17 in single Berlin. Knit 6 rounds and cast off. These are very thick and warm. For a smaller size, cast on for No. 1 in Fingering and work 13 welts; or cast on for No. 2 in single Berlin and work 15 welts. For a doll, cast 8 stitches on to each of 3 needles in single Berlin and work 9 welts, 4 rounds wide.

No. 2. *Cuffs* ribbed in rounds.

Four needles 12, 4 ply Fingering; or needles 13, single Berlin.

Cast on for No. 4 in the scale in Fingering, or for No. 5 in single Berlin. Rib in ones or in twos for the length in the scale. No. 4 can be ribbed in threes or in fours. For a smaller size, work No. 2 of the scale in Fingering, or No. 3 in single Berlin. For a doll, cast 8 stitches on to each of 3 needles in single Berlin and rib 24 rounds in ones.

The larger cuffs throughout are for men, the smaller are for women and children; 2 ozs. of 4 ply Fingering will make 3 of the larger pairs, except the welted ones, for which 1¼ oz. of Fingering is needed for a pair, rather less of single Berlin will be enough in each case. To make the doll's cuffs smaller, use needles 14 and Andalusian. Needles one size smaller are used for the ribbing, because it produces looser work than welting does.

Standard IV.

Four needles 13 2½ ozs of 4 ply Fingering for a pair.

Work *a sock*, size 3 of the scale It will fit a boy 11 or 12 years old

STANDARD V.

Four needles 14, 3¾ ozs. of Welsh yarn for a pair.

Work *a sock*, size 4 of the scale. Rib the top in twos and the rest in knit 3 and purl 1. It will fit a boy 12 or 13 years old. Finer needles and yarn, and ribbing throughout the sock are begun here.

STANDARDS VI. & VII.

Four needles 13, 6 ozs. of 4 ply Fingering for a pair.

Work *a stocking*, size 2 of the scale. It will fit a girl 10 or 11 years old.

PUPIL TEACHERS.

Four needles 14, 3 ply Fingering.

1st year, *a sock*; 2nd year, *a stocking*.

A very superior pair of socks and stockings can be knitted by a pupil teacher shewing the following advantages, though they are not needed for the Code it is most useful to be able to work them and teach them correctly. The hose can be ribbed throughout in knit 3 and purl 1, they can also be striped in 2 colours. 1. The top ribbing upside down for socks and a notched hem for stockings. 2. The loose heel. 3. The heel strengthened with a second yarn. 4. The ribbing tapering to a point in the heel. 5. The instep and sole divided. 6. The size and initial marked in the sole. 7. The ribbing tapering to a point in the toe.

SLATE RUBBERS.

Two needles 11, ½ or ¾ oz. of Cotton 6; or needles 12, Cotton 8.

Cast on 38 or 50 stitches. Knit 60 or 72 rows plain; or work a close repeating design that has 2, 3, 4 or 6 stitches in a pattern, see contents in each book; in this case slip the first stitch and knit the last in every row.

BABIES' VESTS.

Two pins 10, 3 ply Lady Betty, Andalusian; or pins 11, 2 ply Lady Betty, Shetland.

Work these by the directions and the scales for ordinary vests, sizes 1 to 3, see contents.

SKULL CAPS.

No. 1. Six needles 15, ¾ oz. of Filoselle.

Cast 50 stitches on to each of the first two needles and 60 on to the third, making a total of 160.

Rib 15 rounds in fives, knit 4 rounds, rib 14 rounds in fives beginning with purling, knit 4 rounds, rib 14 rounds in fives, knit 4 rounds. The ribs here will be over the furrows. Divide the stitches equally on to five needles, making 32 on each. Use a sixth needle and reduce at each end of each needle 10 times with 2 plain rounds after each reducing one, and 5 times with 1 plain round after each,* leaving 10 stitches, put the Filoselle through them and fasten off. To make these reductions put the inner stitch over the outer one, then knit the outer one.

No. 2. Six needles 14, ½ oz. of Andalusian.

Cast 50 stitches on to each of the first two needles and 40 on to the third, making a total of 140.

Rib 13 rounds in fives, knit 4 rounds, rib 12 rounds in fives beginning with purling, knit 4 rounds, rib 12 rounds in fives, knit 4 rounds. Divide the stitches equally on to five needles, making 28 on each. Reduce at each end of each needle 8 times with 2 plain rounds after each reducing one, and 5 times with 1 plain round after each. Finish as from * in No. 1.

No. 3. Six needles 13, ¾ oz. of single Berlin.

Cast 40 stitches on to each of three needles, making a total of 120.

Rib 11 rounds in fives, knit 4 rounds, rib 10 rounds in fives beginning with purling, knit 4 rounds, rib 10 rounds in fives, knit 4 rounds. Divide the stitches equally on to five needles, making 24 on each. Reduce at each end of each needle 6 times with 2 plain rounds after each reducing one, and 5 times with 1 plain round after each. Finish as from * in No. 1.

No. 4. Six needles 12, ¾ oz. of 4 ply Fingering.

Cast 30 stitches on to each of the first two needles and 40 on to the third, making a total of 100.

Rib 9 rounds in fives, knit 4 rounds, rib 8 rounds in fives beginning with purling, knit 4 rounds, rib 8 rounds in fives, knit 4 rounds. Divide the stitches equally on to five needles, making 20 on each. Reduce at each end of each needle 6 times with 2 plain rounds after each reducing one, and 3 times with 1 plain round after each. Finish as from * in No. 1.

No. 5. Six needles 11, 1¼ oz. of double Berlin.

Cast 30 stitches on to each of three needles, making a total of 90.

Rib 7 rounds in threes, knit 4 rounds, rib 6 rounds in threes beginning with purling, knit 4 rounds, rib 6 rounds in threes, knit 4 rounds. Divide the stitches equally on to five needles, making 18 on each. Reduce at each end of each needle 5 times with 2 plain rounds after each reducing one, and 3 times with 1 plain round after each. Finish as from * in No. 1.

These caps can be made larger by casting 10 more stitches on to one needle and by adding 2 or 3 more rounds to each band of ribbing. When made in black, they are useful for Clergymen and Officials in Church or at funerals, and in colours, for long journeys or draughty offices, and the use of them will often prevent influenza, etc. Being very elastic they take the shape of the head better than velvet, silk, etc.

DOLLS' SOCKS.

Four needles 16, Andalusian ; or needles 17, Shetland.

Work these by the directions and the large scale for hose; rib the top in ones, omit the reductions in the heel flap and mark the size in the sole. They can be made very pretty by using a repeating design, see under Babies' first socks. These are acceptable presents to little girls old enough to appreciate their shape and construction.

MITTENS.

Four needles 12, 5 ply Fingering, Alloa; or needles 13, 1¼ to 2¼ ozs. of 4 ply Fingering for a pair; or needles 14, 3 ply Fingering, single Berlin; or needles 15, Andalusian; or needles 16, Shetland, Filoselle; or needles 17, Silk.

The figures refer to No. 3 of the scale.

Cast 18 stitches on to each of the first two needles and 16 on to the third, making a total of 52. Rib 40 rounds in ones or twos. Sizes 2, 5 and 8 can be ribbed here in threes, and sizes 2, 4, 6, 8 and 10 can be ribbed in fours. Knit 14 rounds plain, but in the second of those after the third stitch, purl alternate ones 3 times to mark the size. In the next round begin to increase for the thumb thus: make one by knitting into the back and then into the front of the first stitch, finish the round; in the next round knit the new stitch or stitches, make one as before in the next stitch, that is, the first of those that were cast on, finish the round; knit a round plain. Repeat these three rounds till there are 20 extra stitches on the first needle, twenty fewer than the rounds in the wrist, so making a long sharp pointed gusset or V-shaped addition for the thumb, with increasings on each side of it; in doing this it is well to put some of the hand stitches on to the second and third needles to equalise the number, but the position of the thumb stitches must not be altered; the last of the thumb rounds will be a plain one. The first of each pair of these extra stitches will be on the right side of the V, that is, it will be the first stitch in the round; the second of each pair will be on the left or second side of the V, that is, it will be the last of the thumb stitches, and will be made by increasing in the first of the hand stitches, namely, those that were cast on at the wrist. The number of rounds in the thumb will be 30, half as many more as the number of stitches in the thumb, as there are three rounds for two increasings. Any letter or figure can be worked in the palm by purling the stitches according to a sampler. The number of stitches on the needles will be 72. Put the thumb stitches on to a piece of cotton, restore the hand stitches to their original needles, and knit them plain for 8 rounds, making the gusset thus: cast 8 stitches on to the third needle, at the end of the last of the rounds in the thumb; make the circle and knit the new stitches plain in the first of the 8 rounds, then in every alternate round, knit the first two together and the last two together of the new stitches, till only those are left that were cast on at the wrist, namely, 52; finish the 8 plain rounds, rib 10 rounds in ones and cast off. Divide the 20 thumb stitches equally on to three needles, knit them plain for 8 rounds, making the gusset thus: knit up 8 stitches on the first needle from those 8 extra ones that were cast on for the hand gusset, leaving an end nine inches long to draw up the corners, work as before directed, till only the 20 thumb stitches are left; finish the 8 plain rounds, rib 10 rounds in ones and cast off. After the wrist ribbing is finished all the sizes can be worked in Roma 2, or thus: knit two rounds plain, then knit one and purl one all round; repeat those three rounds, working the thumb and gussets as before directed. The design can be made in the thumb by keeping the purled stitches over each other; to do this begin the first pattern round in the thumb by knitting one and the next by purling one, in the latter case the last thumb stitch must be knitted as well as the first hand stitch. They also can be ribbed throughout in knit 3 and purl 1, the last stitch in each round being a purled one; when beginning the thumb put the first stitch in the round, which is a knitted one, back on to the third needle, and begin to increase in the middle stitch of the rib, thus making a margin on each side of the V; in the fifth round purl the third new stitch and each one above it to keep the rib straight, also purl the fourth stitches on each side of this one as they arise; keep the purled stitches over each other all round; work the gussets as before directed, after the one in the hand is finished restore the displaced stitch to the first needle, to avoid dividing a rib. Turn the mitten and darn the corners of the gussets.

Size 4 made in Andalusian by a medium knitter will fit over a kid glove size $6\frac{1}{4}$ to $6\frac{3}{4}$. They can be made to match the dress or its trimmings. Work a much shorter wrist for men. It is well to mark the R.H. mitten with contrasting wool, at the front edge of the wrist, to distinguish it.

A *combined cuff and mitten* can be made by ribbing for the wrist twice the length in the scale; the first half can be coloured if the mittens are black, or vice-versâ; if a frilled edge is preferred for the cuff work thus : knit the mitten by the scale, then knit up at its wrist edge as many stitches as were cast on there, rib the same length, then work the frill, see under Cuffs, turn it back over the hand; these are very thick and warm.

BATH OR WASHING SQUARES.

In all these squares slip the first stitch and knit the last in every row. Work them in a close repeating design that has 2, 3, 4 or 6 stitches in a pattern, see contents in each book. The use of them saves the corners of the chamber towels from wear and makes a more wholesome friction for the skin than flannel.

No. 1. Fine.

Two needles 12, ½ or ¾ oz. of Cotton 8.

Cast on 62 or 74 stitches. Work 84 or 96 rows.

No 2. Medium.

Two needles 11, ¾ or 1 oz. of Cotton 6.

Cast on 50 or 62 stitches. Work 72 or 84 rows.

No. 3. Coarse.

Two needles 10, 1 or 1½ oz. of Cotton 4.

Cast on 38 or 50 stitches. Work 60 or 72 rows.

These look well with a margin of plain knitting all round the edge, 2 or 3 inches wide, the centre being worked in a close repeating design.

BATH OR WASHING GLOVES.

Four needles 10, 1 to 1¾ oz. of Cotton 4 for one glove; or needles 11, Cotton 6; or needles 12, Cotton 8.

Work these by the directions and the scale for Babies' gloves, No. 2, see contents; omit the holes round the wrist, work 20 more plain rounds in the hand and 10 more in the thumb in every size, and in every third round after the ribbing at the wrist knit 1 and purl 1 all round to make a rough surface.

LAUNDRY BLUE BAGS.

Four needles 11, ½ oz. of Cotton 6, navy blue, unbleached or white, 4 ply Fingering; or needles 12, Cotton 8, 3 ply Fingering, single Berlin.

Cast 12 or 16 stitches on to each of three needles, making a total of 36 or 48. Rib 8 or 12 rounds in twos. Make 1 and knit 2 together all round, this will make holes for the tape, knit a round. Work 20 or 28 rounds in Roma 1 or Huckaback 2, see contents. In the next round, on each needle, knit or purl the first 2 stitches together and the last 2 together; work a round without reducing, still continuing the design; repeat these 2 rounds till there are 12 stitches, put the yarn through them and fasten off. Run in the tape, knot a loop in the middle of it one inch long, by which to hang up the bag. These bags are very pretty for Christmas trees, made in bright coloured wool: for children, with a small coin put in or filled with tiny biscuits; for their mothers, filled with a collection of buttons, etc.

These make good *money or sample bags ;* cast 4 or 8 stitches more on to each needle, and work 8 or 12 more rounds before reducing; the School cotton is suitable, use different colours for different accounts, and fine braid instead of tape.

BLACKBOARD RUBBERS.

Two needles 10, 1¼ or 1½ oz. of Cotton 4; or needles 11, Cotton 6.

Cast on 50 or 62 stitches. Knit 72 or 84 rows plain; or work a close repeating design that has 2, 3, 4 or 6 stitches in a pattern, see contents in each book; in this case slip the first stitch and knit the last in every row.

FLOOR RUBBERS.

Two pins 4, 4, 5½ or 7 ozs. of Scouring cotton.

Cast on 26, 32 or 38 stitches. Slip the first stitch and knit the last in every row. Work 60, 66 or 72 rows in Huckaback 2, Roma 1, or any close repeating design that has 2, 3, or 6 stitches in a pattern, see contents in each book. Size 1 is 9 inches by 13, and size 3 is 12 by 17.

F

VESTS.

Two pins 8, 4 ply Fingering, 3 ply Fleecy; or pins 9, 3 ply Fingering, 2 ply Fleecy, 1¼ to 5¾ ozs. of single Berlin, 4 ply Lady Betty, Angola 8; or pins 10, 2 ply Fingering, ¾ to 3¼ ozs. of Andalusian, 3 ply Lady Betty, Angola 10; or pins 11, Shetland, 2 ply Lady Betty. For dolls, pins 11, Andalusian; or pins 12, Shetland.

The figures refer to No. 3 of the scales.

No. 1. Ribbed in Ones.

Cast on 57 stitches. Knit twelve rows plain, that is, six ridges, but in the seventh row after the fourth stitch, make one and knit two together 3 times to mark the size. Row 13. Knit 4, * knit 1, purl 1, repeat from *, at the end knit 5. Row 14. Knit 4, * purl 1, knit 1, repeat from *, at the end purl 1, knit 4. Repeat these last two rows till 72 are done. Knit twelve rows, but in the seventh row after the second stitch, knit one and make one and knit two together to the end, this will make holes round the neck for the ribbon; finish the twelve rows and cast off. Work the front without marking the size. The right side of each piece is that in which ribs, not furrows, are next to the margin. For the shoulder strap, cast on 20 stitches; knit 12 rows plain, but after working half the number, make ribbon holes as before, finish the 12 rows and cast off. For the gusset, cast on 13 stitches; knit four rows plain, then reduce in every row by knitting the second and third stitches together till there are three, knit them together. Sew up the sides beginning from the lower edge, leaving enough for the armholes, sew in the arm gussets, then sew the ends of the straps to the top of the body.

No. 2. Ribbed in Twos.

Cast on 58 stitches. Row 1. Knit 4, * knit 2, purl 2, repeat from *, at the end knit 6. Row 2. Knit 4, * purl 2, knit 2, repeat from *, at the end purl 2, knit 4. Repeat these two rows till 6 are done Knit 24 rows plain, that is, twelve ridges, but in the third row after the fourth stitch, make one and knit two together 3 times to mark the size. Rib 70 rows as before. * In the next row knit 12 for the first shoulder strap, knit the outer four stitches on each side of it plain, but rib the middle ones throughout each strap; cast off 34 stitches and one more, leaving one fewer on the L.H.N. than the number in the strap, which with the one on the R.H.N. will make 12 for the other strap; knit three, rib in twos except the last four stitches, which four knit plain; knit 16 rows and cast off, there will be eight ridges above the level of the neck. Continue the first strap to match, beginning the row, which will be the second one, at the neck side. Work the front without marking the size. The right side of each piece is that in which ribs, not furrows, are next to the margin. For the sleeve, cast on 10 stitches; knit 84 rows plain, that is, forty-two ridges, and cast off. Sew the strap ends together; then form the gusset of the sleeve by sewing one end of the piece to one of its sides, close to the opposite end, this will make a two-fold triangle, put this join at the back of the vest, that is, where the size is marked, then join the sides beginning from the lower edge. The weight of size 9 is for Shetland and of size 10 for Andalusian.

No. 3. With a Border.

Cast on 58 stitches. Slip the first stitch and knit the last in every row. Work 22 border rows in a close or open repeating design that has 2, 4 or 8 stitches in a pattern, see contents in each book. Knit 42 ridges. Finish as from * in No. 2, only knit the shoulder straps plain.

No 4. Ribbed in Fours.

Cast on 60 stitches. Row 1. Knit 8 for the margin, * knit 4, purl 4, repeat from *, at the end knit 4 and 8 for the margin. Row 2. Knit 8 for the margin, * purl 4, knit 4, repeat from *, at the end purl 4 and knit 8 for the margin. Repeat these two rows till 96 are done. A variety can be made by knitting all the stitches on the wrong side at regular intervals; or, put pairs of these cross rows at intervals. There will be 6 ribs on the right side, this will mark the size. Finish as from * in No. 2, put sleeves or gussets as preferred.

All these vests are low bodied and are for children and

women. Work a row of double crochet round all the edges to preserve them, and a row of scallops round the neck for ribbon holes, or, trim the neck and sleeves with a narrow edging, see book 3. Sleeves or gussets can be put to any of them as the different sizes in the four sorts correspond.

BABIES' GLOVES OR MUFFLERS.

Four or five needles 14, ¾ to 1¼ oz. of single Berlin for a pair, 4 ply Lady Betty; or needles 15, Andalusian, 3 ply Lady Betty; or needles 16, Shetland, 2 ply Lady Betty.
The figures refer to No. 3 of the scale.

No. 1. WITHOUT THUMBS.

Cast 14 stitches on to each of the first two needles and 16 on to the third, making a total of 44. Rib 26 rounds in ones or twos. Knit one round plain; then make 2 and knit 2 together all round, and in the next round treat the new double stitches as single ones; this will make holes for the ribbon. Work 44 rounds in Huckaback 2, or Roma 1, see contents. Divide the stitches equally on to four needles, use a fifth needle, and in the next round, on each needle, knit or purl the first two stitches together and the last two together, there will be eight reductions; work a round without reducing, still continuing the design ; repeat these two rounds till there are 12 stitches, put the wool through them and fasten off.

No. 2. WITH THUMBS.

Cast 14 stitches on to each of the first two needles and 16 on to the third, making a total of 44. Rib 26 rounds in ones or twos. Knit one round plain; then make 2 and knit 2 together all round, and in the next round treat the new double stitches as single ones; this will make holes for the ribbon. Knit 9 rounds plain, but in the second of these after the third stitch, purl alternate ones 3 times to mark the size. In the next round begin to increase for the thumb thus: make one by knitting into the back of the first stitch, knit into the front of it and finish the round; in the next round knit the new stitch or stitches, make one by knitting into the back of the next stitch, that is, the first of those that were cast on, knit into the front of it and finish the round; knit the next round plain. Repeat these three rounds till there are 16 extra stitches on the first needle, so making a V-shaped addition for the thumb, with increasings on each side of it; the last of the thumb rounds will be a plain one. The number of rounds in the thumb will be 24 and the number of stitches on the needles will be 60. Put the thumb stitches on to a piece of cotton, knit the hand stitches plain for 16 rounds, making the gusset thus: cast 6 stitches on to the third needle, at the end of the last of the rounds in the thumb; make the circle and knit the new stitches plain in the first of the 16 rounds, then, in every alternate round, knit the first two together and the last two together of the new stitches, till only those stitches are left that were cast on at the wrist; finish the 16 plain rounds. Halve the stitches by keeping a quarter on the first needle, a quarter on the second and half on the third. On the first needle knit one, knit two together, knit to the end; on the second needle knit to within three stitches of the end, knit two together, knit one; on the third needle knit one, knit two together, knit to within three stitches of the end, knit two together, knit one. This will make a reduction at each end of each side and will lessen the number of stitches by four in each reducing round. There are to be 5 of these reducing rounds with two plain ones after each. The number of stitches now on the needles will be 24. Turn the glove inside out, put the stitches that are on the first two needles on to one, then cast off double, knitting the first four stitches together and the last four together, to make it less square. Divide the thumb stitches equally on to three needles, knit them plain for 12 rounds, making the gusset thus: knit up 6 extra stitches on to the first needle, from those 6 extra ones that were cast on for the hand gusset, work as before directed till only the 16 thumb stitches are left; finish the plain rounds, then knit two together and knit three all round, till there are from six to eight stitches, put the wool through them and fasten off. These are very pretty worked in Roma 2, see contents.

CHEST WRAPS.

Two pins 5, 4 ply Fingering, 3 ply Fleecy; or pins 6, single Berlin, 2 ply Fleecy.
The figures refer to No. 3 of the scale.

Cast on 25 stitches. Knit 6 ridges, but in the seventh row of them work thus: knit four, make two, knit two together, knit to within five stitches of the end, make two, knit two together, knit three, this will make two holes; in the next row treat the new double stitches as single ones. Increase in the fourth stitch in every row by knitting into the back and then into the front of it till there are 105 stitches. Knit 14 ridges, without increasing. In the next row knit 38 for the first shoulder, put them on to a piece of string, cast off for the neck leaving one stitch fewer for this shoulder than in the first one, with these 38 stitches * knit 50 ridges; then reduce in every row by knitting the fourth and fifth stitches together till there are five, and cast off. Continue the first shoulder to match, beginning the row, which will be the second one, at the neck side, repeat from *. Sew half a yard of ribbon on to each point narrow enough to go through the holes at the waist and tie there. Work a row of double crochet round the neck to preserve the edge. The weight of size 6 is for single Berlin.

GARTERS.

Two needles 13, 1½ oz. of Cotton 8, or 1¼ oz. of single Berlin for a pair.

Cast on 7 stitches. Increase in the second stitch in every row by knitting into the back and then into the front of it till there are 14 stitches. Knit 280 ridges plain. Reduce in every row by knitting the second and third stitches together till there are 7 and cast off. An insertion can be used, see contents in each book. A *loop* can be made at the end thus: instead of reducing knit the first 7 stitches for 30 ridges, leaving the rest on the needle. Fold this strap and with a third needle cast off double with the stitches that were left on the needle, beginning from the outer edge.

LEGGINGS.

Four needles 10, 4 ply Fingering, 3 ply Fleecy; or needles 11, 3 ply Fingering, 2 ply Fleecy.

Work these by the directions for stockings, cast off loosely after the ankle ribbing. They are very useful for cold and long journeys, or for walking in the rain and snow.

BALLS.

Four needles 11, 4 ply Fingering, 3 ply Fleecy; or needles 12, 3 ply Fingering, 2 ply Fleecy, single Berlin.

Cast 12 or 16 stitches on to each of three needles, making a total of 36 or 48. Rib 21 or 30 rounds in ones, twos or threes, in 3 or 5 strips of bright contrasting colours. Cast on and cast off tightly. Gather one end and fasten it, fill it with anything light and elastic, put a small box into the middle with some dried peas in it as a rattle, gather the other end and fasten it. These form good *oranges* for Christmas trees, made in yellow wool and Huckaback 1 or 2, see contents.

FRINGES.

No. 1. FINGER.

Cast on 5 stitches. Row 1. Slip 1, knit 2, make 1, knit 2 together. Row 2. Wind the yarn 3 or 4 times round 3 or 4 fingers, according to the thickness and length needed; knit all these into the first stitch and treat them as one stitch in the next row, then knit 1, make 1, knit 2 together, knit 1.

No. 2. TUFT.

Cast on 8 stitches. Row 1. Knit 2, make 1 and knit 2 together twice, hang on to the yarn close to the R.H.N. 3 or 4 pieces of it twice as long as the depth of fringe needed, put the tuft forward, knit 1, put it back, knit 1. Row 2. Knit. To cut the pieces for this fringe, wind the yarn round a stiff book that will measure just the length needed, then cut through the groove in its front.

No. 3. Unravelled.

1st. Cast on any number of stitches. Knit plain for the length needed. Cast off 3 or 4 stitches and unravel the rest.

2nd. Cast on 6 or 8 stitches. Row 1. Make 1 and purl 2 together to the end. Every row is the same. Cast off 2 or 4 stitches and unravel the rest.

3rd. Cast on 8 stitches. Row 1. Knit 2, make 1, knit 2 together, knit 1, make 1, knit 2 together, knit 1. Every row is the same. Cast off 5 stitches and unravel the rest.

4th. Cast on 12 stitches. Row 1. Knit 2, make 1 and knit 2 together twice, knit 6. Row 2. Knit 7, make 1 and knit 2 together twice, knit 1. Cast off the 6 pattern stitches and unravel the rest.

All these fringes can be cut, crossed and knotted at regular intervals.

PATCHWORK SHAPES.

Two needles 10, double Berlin, 4 ply Fleecy, Cotton 4; or needles 11, 4 ply Fingering, 3 ply Fleecy, Cotton 6; or needles 12, 3 ply Fingering, single Berlin, 2 ply Fleecy, Cotton 8; or needles 13, Andalusian, Cotton 10.

These shapes serve for using up short pieces of yarn to make coverlets, etc., the light and bright pieces should be divided by others of a dark, plain colour.

No. 1. Square.

Cast on 22 or 30 stitches. Slip the first stitch and knit the last in every row. Work 30 or 36 rows in Huckaback 2 or Roma 1, see contents, and cast off.

No. 2. Triangle.

Cast on 22 or 30 stitches. Knit a row, then reduce in every row by knitting the second and third stitches together till there are 3, knit them together.

No. 3. Sexagon.

Cast on 8 or 12 stitches. Increase in the second stitch in every row by knitting into the back and then into the front of it till there are 20 or 30 stitches; then reduce in every row by knitting the second and third stitches together till there are 8 or 12 and cast off.

No. 4. DIAMOND.

Cast on 2 stitches. Increase in the second stitch in the first 2 rows by knitting into the back and then into the front of it, knit 2 rows plain; repeat these 4 rows till there are 16 or 20 stitches. Reduce in the next 2 rows by knitting the second and third stitches together, knit 2 rows plain; repeat these 4 rows till there are 2 stitches, knit them together.

KETTLE OR IRON HOLDERS.

No. 1. PLAIN.

Two needles 10, ¾ or 1 oz. of 4 ply Fleecy, double Berlin: or needles 11, 4 ply Fingering, 3 ply Fleecy.

Cast on 26 or 38 stitches. Slip the first stitch and knit the last in every row. Work 56 or 18 rows in a close repeating design that has 2, 3, 4 or 6 stitches in a pattern, see contents in each book. Three of these squares are needed. Bind them together with braid, line it and put a tab.

No. 2. FLUTED.

Two needles 10, ¾ oz of black and 1 oz. of coloured double Berlin, 4 ply Fleecy; or needles 11, ⅔ oz. of 4 ply Fingering, 3 ply Fleecy.

Cast on tightly 49 or 63 stitches with the coloured wool. Knit a row. In the next row knit 7 stitches with the coloured wool and 7 with the black alternately, finishing with the coloured. Knit thus in rows till there are 36 or 40 ridges in the margin; keep the wools crossed on one side of the work very tight to make the two colours rise in flutes, and in every row twist the wools together twice before beginning the first flute. With the coloured wool knit a row on the right side of the work and cast off. Gather each end, add bows of ribbon to match the wool, line it and put a tab.

G

BATH TOWELS.

In all the strips for these towels slip the first stitch and knit the last in every row. Knit 2 rows plain; in the third row knit 1 and make 1 and knit 2 together to the end, this will make holes for the fringe; knit a row plain; work the right length in a close repeating design that has 2, 3, 4 or 6 stitches in a pattern, see contents in each book; work a row of holes; knit 2 rows plain and cast off. For the fringe, knot 3 or 4 pieces of the same cotton, 10 inches long, into every hole. In joining the cotton put the knot at the edge of the strip that the ends may be sewn in. Work a row of double crochet along each outer edge of the towel to preserve the knitting.

No. 1. Fine. In 5 Strips.

Two needles 12, 13 ozs. of cotton 8.

Cast on 50 stitches. Work 450 rows. Five of these strips are needed. Use three designs that contrast well, one being for the middle and the other two in pairs or in the two parts of one design. This can be made in 1 strip by casting on 242 stitches, or in 3 strips by casting on 74 in each; it will be about 42 inches long by 23 wide.

No. 2. Medium. In 3 Strips.

Two needles 11, 15 ozs. of cotton 6.

Cast on 74 stitches. Work 400 rows. Three of these strips are needed. Use two designs that contrast well, one being for the middle. This can be made in 1 strip by casting on 218 stitches, or in 5 strips by casting on 38 in each; it will be about 44 inches long by 25 wide.

No. 3. Coarse. In 1 Strip.

Two needles 10, $12\frac{1}{2}$ ozs. of cotton 4.

Cast on 122 stitches. Work 300 rows. This can be made in 3 strips by casting on 38 in each, or in 5 strips by casting on 26 in each; it will be about 40 inches long by 21 wide.

These towels make strong, useful *Antimacassars;* use unbleached cotton, or the School cotton, brown and red are suitable. Work the strips in a handsome repeating design or insertion, see contents in each book; alternate narrow and wide strips and close and open designs well contrasted; fringe the ends or sew on an edging all round or at the ends only, see book 3. A very large variety can easily and quickly be made at a small cost.

CUFFS.

Four needles 11, 5 ply Fingering, Alloa; or needles 12, $\frac{1}{2}$ to 1 oz. of 4 ply Fingering for a pair, 3 ply Fleecy; or needles 13, 3 ply Fingering, single Berlin, 2 ply Fleecy; or needles 14, 2 ply Fingering, Andalusian; or needles 15, Shetland, Filoselle; or needles 16, Silk. The figures refer to No. 3 of the scale.

No. 1. RIBBED.

Cast 14 stitches on to each of the first two needles and 16 on to the third, making a total of 44. Rib 48 rounds in ones or twos and cast off. Sizes 1, 4, 7 and 10 can be ribbed in threes, and sizes 2, 4, 6, 8 and 10 can be ribbed in fours; in these cases put a multiple of 3 or 4 stitches on to each needle. These cuffs look well in stripes of two colours; or, in two or more shades of one colour; or, the edges of 10 or 12 rounds in a bright colour and the rest in black or brown, etc; or, vice versâ; or, half in one colour and the rest in another; or, the first third and the last third of the length can be ribbed and the middle worked in a close or open repeating design; or, vice versâ.

No. 2. OPEN RIBBED.

Round 1. Knit 2, purl 2; or knit 3, purl 3. Round 2. Knit 2, make 1, purl 2 together; or knit 3, purl 1, make 1, purl 2 together. Repeat these 2 rounds till the cuff is long enough.

No. 3. FRILLED.

For these cuffs use two colours, or two or three shades of one colour. Rib in twos; then, with wool one size finer than that used for the knitting, work a row of double crochet up and down each side and round each end of every rib; on this crochet a row of small scallops or another row of double crochet. The frill should be rather full.

No. 4. Frilled Edge.

All the sizes can be made with a frill at one edge to fall over the hand; work thus: rib in twos for the length in the scale; make all the new stitches by crossing the yarn over the needle; in the next round increase thus: knit 1, make 1, knit 1, purl 1, make 1, purl 1, repeat to the end of the round; rib 3 rounds in threes; increase again thus: knit 1, make 1, knit 1, make 1, knit 1, purl 1, make 1, purl 1, make 1, purl 1, repeat; rib 3 rounds in fives; increase again thus: knit 2, make 1, knit 1, make 1, knit 2, purl 2, make 1, purl 1, make 1, purl 2, repeat; rib 3 rounds in sevens; cast off the second way. The frill can be made narrower by ribbing 2 rounds after each increasing one, or wider by ribbing 4 rounds after each. A second frill, an inch longer, can be added, the two look very handsome; work thus: turn back the first frill over the cuff, knit up the same number of stitches as in the cuff 10 rounds below the beginning of the first frill, then rib 24 rounds in twos and work the frill as before.

No. 5. Double.

To make the cuffs double, rib twice the length in the scale and 10 rounds more; fold the ends into the middle and sew them together, making the ribs meet, put this join inside. These are very warm and fill up the space between the wrist and the sleeve.

No. 6. Fancy Work.

All the sizes can be made in some of the repeating designs, such as Spira, Wave, Hollingsclougth, Doric, *Willow leaf, *Colonia, Hemstitch or *Wavelet, see contents in each book; do not divide a pattern on to two needles.

No. 7. Kilted.

For these cuffs use needles 13, 1¼ oz. of single Berlin, black, brown, cardinal, grey or navy. Cast on for No. 4 in the scale. Work Kilt No. 1, size 3, in rounds, one part for each cuff, see contents; continue till there are 7 triangles in length; rib 10 rounds in twos; then work a frill as above. These will fit a medium sized woman.

COMFORTERS.

Two pins 4, 3½ to 12¼ ozs. of 4 ply Fingering, 3 ply Fleecy; or pins 5, 3 ply Fingering, 2 ply Fleecy, single Berlin, 4 ply Lady Betty; or pins 6, 2 ply Fingering, Andalusian, 3 ply Lady Betty; or pins 7, Shetland, 2 ply Lady Betty; or pins 8, Pyrenees.
The figures refer to No. 3 of the scale.

Cast on 62 stitches. Slip the first stitch and knit the last in every row. Knit two rows plain; in the third row knit 1 and make 1 and knit 2 together to the end, this will make holes for the fringe; knit a row plain. Knit 170 ridges plain, or work the right length in a close or open repeating design that has 2, 3, 4, 6 or 12 stitches in a pattern, see contents in each book; work a row of holes; knit two rows plain and cast off. For the fringe, knot 3 or 4 pieces of the same wool, 10 inches long, into every hole; the small sizes can be finished with large tassels and the ends of the large ones can be trimmed with an edging, see book 3. If plain margins are preferred work thus: for the small sizes, knit the first 4 stitches and the last 4 plain, in every row, leaving a multiple of 6 for the design; for the large sizes, knit the first 7 stitches and the last 7 plain, in every row, leaving a multiple of 12 for the design. They can be worked in *welts*, 6, 8 or 10 rows wide, see contents, when casting off drop every sixth or twelfth stitch, except the last one, and let them run down the whole length to make Jacob's ladders; these can be made in two colours. They also look very pretty made in *spaces*, thus: work from 16 to 24 rows in a small open design, such as Hemstitch, and then knit from 5 to 10 ridges plain or work a small close design for the same length, such as Huckaback or Roma; alternate these spaces for the length needed, the first and last spaces must be alike and both must have from 4 to 10 more rows than are in the rest to make them appear the same length; or, work all the length in an open design, putting three wide bands of a close design or of plain knitting at each end divided by 6 or 8 rows of the open one. Size 1 is about 8 inches wide by 46 long, and size 6 about 23 inches by 68, both made in 4 ply Fingering; 5¼ ozs. of 3 ply Fingering will make size 6.

BABIES' FIRST SOCKS.

Four needles 15, 2 ply Fingering, Andalusian, 3 ply Lady Betty, Angola and Cotton 10; or needles 16, Filoselle, 2 ply Lady Betty, Shetland, Angola and Cotton 12; or needles 17, Silk, Angola and Cotton and Crochet cotton 14; or needles 18, Angola and Cotton and Crochet cotton 16.

Work these by the directions and the scale for socks, sizes 0 to 4. Omit the seam stitch when casting on and add it when the top ribbing is ended; rib the top in ones and mark the size in the sole. For the rest of the sock, purl every fourth or fifth round; or, rib in knit 2 and purl 1; or, cross the ribbing at regular intervals by purling every fourth or fifth round; or, in every fourth or fifth round knit 2 or 3, make 1 and knit 2 together, repeat this in the front only; or, work welts in the front only; or, work a close or open repeating design, see contents in each book; omit the leg reducings if advisable, continue the ribs, etc. half way down the heel and in the instep to the toe reducings. A welt can be put in the leg after the top ribbing; or, a round of holes, made thus: knit 2, make 1, knit or purl 2 together, repeat to the end.

BABIES' LEGGINGS.

Four needles 11, single Berlin, 4 ply Lady Betty; or needles 12, Andalusian, 3 ply Lady Betty.

Work these by the directions for stockings, and by the scale for ordinary leggings, sizes 1 to 3, cast off loosely after the ankle ribbing. They can be made very pretty by using a close repeating design, see under Babies' first socks.

BRACES.

Two needles 15, ¾ or 1 oz. of Cotton 8.

Cast on 20 or 26 stitches. Work tightly throughout; knit the first 4 stitches and the last 4 plain in every row. Work the middle stitches in a close repeating design that has 2, 3, 4, or 6 stitches in a pattern, or, use an insertion, see contents in each book; continue till there are 120 or 130 ridges in the margin and cast off. Two of these strips are needed. Cross them for the back and stitch them there then add the usual leather ends.

HAND MUFFLERS.

Four needles 12, Alloa; or needles 13, 1¼ to 2¾ ozs. of 4 ply Fingering for a pair, 3 ply Fleecy; or needles 14, 3 ply Fingering, 2 ply Fleecy, single Berlin; or needles 15, Andalusian.

Work these by the directions and the scale for Babies' gloves, No. 2, see contents; omit the holes round the wrist, work 20 more plain rounds in the hand and 10 more in the thumb in every size; knit plain, or work a close repeating design that has 2 or 4 stitches in a pattern, Roma 2 is most suitable. These mufflers or Canadian gloves are useful to wear over other gloves when extra warmth is needed, or for wounded or rheumatic hands.

NIGHT CAPS.
No. 1. PLAIN.

Four needles 13, 1¾ or 2¼ ozs. of 4 ply Fingering, Cotton 6; or needles 14, 1¼ or 1½ oz. of single Berlin, Cotton 8.

Cast on 46, 46 and 44 stitches, making a total of 136; or 48, 48, and 48, making a total of 144. Rib 30 rounds in twos. Knit 50 or 60 rounds plain. In the next round reduce by knitting 2 together at 6 stitches from each end of each of the three needles, knit a round plain; repeat these two rounds till there are 42 stitches; then knit 2 together and knit 3 alternately till there are 10 stitches, put the yarn through them and fasten off. Work a row of double crochet, quite loosely, round the edge.

No. 2. SQUARE CROWNED.

Five needles 13, 2¾ ozs. of 4 ply Fingering.

Cast 2 stitches on to each of four needles making a total of 8. Round 1. Knit 1, make 1, knit 1, on each needle. Round 2. Knit plain. Round 3. Knit 1, make 1, knit all but the last, make 1, knit 1, on each needle. Round 4. Knit plain. Repeat these last 2 rounds till there are 140 or 148 stitches. Knit 70 or 90 rounds plain. Rib 30 rounds in twos and cast off. Work a row of double crochet, quite loosely, round the edge.

This makes a good *boating cap;* use two colours, well contrasted, or two shades of one colour; knit 5 or 10 rounds of each alternately; or, 3 rounds of one colour and 7 of the other; or, any other pretty variety.

NECK TIES.

No. 1. PLAIN. IN ROUNDS.

Four needles 14, 1½ or 2 ozs. of Filoselle.

Cast 16 or 20 stitches on to each of three needles, making a total of 48 or 60. Rib 30 rounds in twos. Knit 36 or 38 inches plain; rib 30 rounds in twos and cast off. It will be double, and 40 or 42 inches long by 1¼ or 2 inches wide. This is for tying in a knot.

No. 2. BRIOCHE. IN ROWS.

Two needles 16, 1¼ or 1½ oz. of Filoselle.

Cast on 30 or 36 stitches. Work 40 or 42 inches in Brioche, see contents, and cast off. It will be single and 2 or 2½ inches wide. This is for putting through a ring.

NIGHT OR SLEEPING SOCKS.

Four needles 11, 5 ply Fingering, 4 ply Fleecy, double Berlin; or needles 12, 4 ply Fingering, 3 ply Fleecy; or needles 13, 3 ply Fingering, 2 ply Fleecy, single Berlin.

Work these by the directions and the large scale for hose. Use undyed, scarlet or white wool.

DUSTERS.

Two needles 10, Cotton 4; or needles 11, 4½ ozs. of Cotton 6; or needles 12, Cotton 8.

No. 1. In 4 squares. Cast on 62 stitches. Slip the first stitch and knit the last in every row. Work 84 rows in a close repeating design that has 2, 3, 4 or 6 stitches in a pattern, see contents in each book. Four of these squares are needed. Use two designs that contrast well and sew them together so that different ones may be side by side.

No. 2. In 3 strips. Cast on 38 stitches. Slip the first stitch and knit the last in every row. Work 156 rows in a close repeating design that has 2, 3, 4 or 6 stitches in a pattern, see contents in each book. Three of these strips are needed. Use two designs that contrast well, one being for the middle. This can be made in one strip by casting on 110 stitches; it is smaller than the preceding one.

STAYS FOR CHILDREN AND DOLLS.

Two needles 13, 1¼ to 4 ozs. of Cotton 6; or for winter, 4 ply Fingering, 2¼ ozs. for size 5. For dolls, needles 14, ¼ oz. of Cotton 8 for one of each size.

The figures refer to No. 3 of the scale.

Cast on 60 stitches. Knit 92 rows plain for the back, that is, forty-six ridges. * Cast off 14 stitches, leaving 46 on the L.H.N. and one on the R.H.N; this is to form the arm hole. Knit 18 shorter rows. If a *gusset* for the hip is needed work thus: knit half the shorter rows, in the next row knit the first four stitches beginning from the lower edge, turn and knit them again, so making a ridge four stitches long ; knit six, turn and knit them again; continue knitting in short ridges, increasing their length by including two more stitches each time of turning till 14 are used for the height of the gusset, the other stitches in the arm hole row remaining on the R.H.N.; to make the other half of the gusset, leave two stitches on the R.H.N. every time of turning till there are four on the L.H.N.; knit them the second time, then knit the whole arm hole row and finish the rest of them. At the end of these shorter rows cast on thirteen stitches to restore the number originally cast on. * Knit 152 rows plain for the front, that is, seventy-six ridges, then work again from * to *. Knit 92 rows plain for the other back and cast off. If button holes are preferred to tape work thus : in the fifth row from the end, beginning from the upper edge, knit three, then cast off five and knit five alternately to the end of the row ; in the next row cast on four stitches at every hole to restore the number, then finish the back. For the shoulder strap, cast on 7 stitches, knit 52 rows, that is, twenty-six ridges and cast off; leave cotton at both ends to sew it on to the body. Work a row of double crochet round all the edges to preserve them. Back the inside of both ends with wide tape, sew on the buttons, cut the holes in the tape and work them closely with the knitting. If tapes are used for tying, a second piece can be sewn on to one side, further from the end, so as to let them out when needed.

H

BOOTAKINS.

Four needles 11, 3 ply Fingering, 4 ply Lady Betty, single Berlin, or needles 12, 2 ply Fingering, 3 ply Lady Betty, Andalusian.
The figures refer to No. 3 of the scale.

No. 1. In rounds. Work these by the directions and the large scale for hose; rib the top in ones or twos; knit the rest plain, or, rib in knit 3 and purl 1; make 1 and knit 2 together all round just before dividing for the heel, this will make holes for the ribbon; mark the size in the sole. These are very pretty worked in a repeating design, see under Babies' first socks, page 46.

No. 2. In rows. Work the foot for these by the directions and the scales for babies' *boots*, not socks and shoes; any of the sizes of No. 1 of each of the sorts can be used, for they all correspond, as will be seen by referring to the *total leg stitches* in each boot scale; the bootakin scale is a continuation of the boot scales, so that a very large and pretty variety can be made, in all the sizes of each, by a judicious arrangement of designs, insertions or ribs. After the ribbon holes are made round the ankle continue thus: work 26 rows in a small close or open design, * Lois or * Clio 1, or the same that has been used in the foot; or, rib the right number of rows in twos and cross the ribbing by knitting every sixth row except the last, these will be back rows. In the next row knit plain, increasing twice by knitting into the back and then into the front of the first and last stitches, continue knitting plain till there are three ridges, increase as before, work thus till there are ten more stitches, 48 in all, then continue knitting plain till there are 26 ridges in all for the calf. Form the *knee gusset* thus: continue knitting plain, but in every row leave the last stitch unknitted on the L.H.N.; do this till there are 22 middle stitches over the knee, and 13 on each side, on as many levels, under it; slip the first stitch in each of these shortening gusset rows, the last of them will be a back one. In the next row knit the middle stitches and the following side ones, turn and knit all these and the other side ones, continue knitting these 48 stitches plain till there are 10 ridges; work a row of ribbon holes as before, knit back plain; rib 14 rows in twos and cast off loosely. Sew up the seams and run in the ribbon, 1½ yard cut into four pieces of two lengths for a pair. The needles and the wools for these bootakins are the same as those used for babies' boots, to enable knitters to produce the same size in both articles; larger needles and yarns can be used to make them thicker and larger; they can also be made in coloured wool for small children to wear over shoes and socks in their perambulators, for this use pins 9, 5 ply Fingering; or pins 10, 4 ply Fingering.

CORALS OR GIMPS.

Two needles 10, 6 ply Fleecy; or needles 11, double Berlin.

No. 1. Cast on 2 stitches. Make 1, knit 2 together. Every row is the same.

No. 2. Cast on 3 stitches. Slip 1, make 1, knit 2 together. Every row is the same.

No. 3. Cast on 3 stitches. Slip 1, purl 1, knit 1. Every row is the same.

These are useful for trimming jackets, etc., and for babies' shoulder ties, also for *watch guards*, made in coarse silk.

KNITTING THAT MAY BE CUT.

Cast on a multiple of 2 and 1 more. Slip 1, * knit 1. purl 1, repeat from *. Every row is the same.

This is useful for men's waistcoats, tea cosies, or for any work that has to be cut, as the stitches do not unravel and run down.

MUFFS.

Two pins 5, 1¾ or 2¼ ozs, of double Berlin. For dolls, needles 14, Andalusian.

Cast on 42 or 48 stitches. Knit the first 3 stitches and the last 3 plain in every row. Work 80 or 88 rows in a small close repeating design that has 2, 3 or 6 stitches in a pattern, see contents in each book; there will be 40 or 44 ridges in the margin. These are for children, they can be made larger by casting on 6 more stitches and working 8 more rows. For dolls, cast on 18 or 24 stitches, and work 50 or 54 rows in Roma 1.

HOODS.

Two pins 8, 1½ to 2¼ ozs. of 4 ply Fingering, 3 ply Fleecy, rather more of grey than of coloured; or pins 9, 3 ply Fingering, 2 ply Fleecy, single Berlin. For dolls, needles 11, Andalusian; or needles 12, Shetland. The figures refer to No. 3 of the scale.

No. 1. Square.

Cast on 74, 86 or 98 stitches. Slip the first stitch and knit the last in every row. Work 54, 60 or 66 rows in a small close or open repeating design that has 2, 3, 4 or 6 stitches in a pattern, see contents in each book. Fold it to make a square, sew up the back leaving about 2 inches open at the bottom, crochet a row of scallops round all the edges, line it with flannel, sew on ribbon strings and add a bow of the same at the top in front. A frill round the front is a great improvement; increase twice only, see under Cuffs 4, page 44. Nearly 1 oz. of 3 ply Fingering is needed for size 3.

No. 2. Horseshoe Back.

Work all the rows in Brioche, see contents.

Cast on 98 stitches with the coloured wool, which will be 32 patterns or ribs, this will mark the size. Slip the first stitch and knit the last in every row. Work 20 rows for the hem, then with the grey wool work 46 rows for the headpiece. In the next row work 34 stitches, then with the coloured wool work the 30 middle stitches in rows, knitting in at the end of every row, with the last of the middle stitches, one of those left at the sides till all are taken in and a horse-shoe back is made, cut off the coloured wool. Keep the outside of the hood towards you and with the grey wool knit up 25 stitches along one side of the back, beginning immediately after the coloured front hem, work through the coloured horse-shoe back, keeping the design right, then knit up 25 stitches along the other side, stopping at the coloured hem; this will make 80 stitches for the curtain. Work 26 rows, still slipping the first stitch and knitting the last one in every row. In the first of these rows make two instead of one in each pattern in the row, in the next row treat these new double stitches as single ones, this will make holes round the neck for elastic or ribbon. With the coloured wool work 20 rows, the same number as in the front hem, and cast off. It is an improvement if the last four of these rows are grey. With the coloured wool work two rows of crochet round all the edges, the second row being scallops. Hem back the coloured front with a little cotton wool under it, tack in a cap border, run narrow ribbon round the neck, or elastic and add wide ribbon strings with a bow on the top and one at the back. It is well to line it with some soft and warm washing material for babies.

THE GUSSET KNEE.

This can be applied to any stocking, but is useful chiefly for cyclists, as it gives more space for the bent knee and thus relieves the strain on that part of the stocking. The size following is No. 3 of the scale. Cast on and work as before directed, see page 11, till as much of the top is done as will reach to just below the knee, then arrange the stitches thus: knit on to the first needle 5 stitches fewer than a quarter of the total number cast on, that will be 17; leave the same number on the third needle and 1 more, namely the seam stitch, that will be 18; these 35 stitches are to be left unworked till the gusset is finished; the remaining 54 will be on the second or middle needle and with them form the gusset thus: alternately knit and purl in rows, to produce stocking work, but in every row leave the last 2 stitches unknitted or unpurled on the L.H.N.; do this till there are about half of the 54 stitches left in the middle in a short row, that will be 26, and a quarter, namely 14, left at each side, on 7 levels; slip the first stitch in each of these shortening rows, the last of them will be a purled one and will finish the gusset. In the next row knit the 26 middle stitches and the following 14 side ones; with a second needle knit the 18 that were left on the third one, purling the seam stitch; with a third needle knit the 17 that were left on the first one and the following 14 side ones; rearrange these 89 stitches according to the scale, continue knitting in rounds and finish the stocking as before directed. If the knee is needed more bent leave only one stitch on the L.H.N. each time of turning.

REPEATING DESIGNS.

No. 1. BARBARA.

Cast on a multiple of 2 and 1 more.
Rows 1 and 3. Knit 1, * purl 1, knit 1, repeat from *.
Row 2 and every alternate one. Purl. Rows 5 and 7.
Purl 1, * knit 1, purl 1, repeat from *.

No. 2. ANNABERG.

Cast on a multiple of 2.
Rounds 1 to 4. Knit. Rounds 5 and 6. Purl. Round 7. Make 1, knit 2 together. Round 8. Knit. Round 9. Like round 7. Round 10. Knit. Rounds 11 and 12. Purl.

No. 3. BRIOCHE.

Cast on a multiple of 3.
Row 1. Make 1, slip 1, knit 2 together. Every row is the same, so both sides are alike. In this design only half the number of rows, in any given length, appears on one side of the work; the other half is composed of the slipped stitches, which sink into the furrow and appear on the other side of the work: thus the right number of rows in the directions or scales is gained by counting half on each side, the ridge of one side being the furrow of the other one.

No. 4. HUCKABACK.

Both sides of each size are alike, they can be worked in rounds.
Size 1. Cast on a multiple of 2.
Row 1. Knit 1, purl 1. Row 2. Purl 1, knit 1.
Size 2. Cast on a multiple of 4.
Rows 1 and 2. Knit 2, purl 2. Rows 3 and 4. Purl 2, knit 2.
Size 3. Cast on a multiple of 6.
Rows 1 to 3. Knit 3, purl 3. Rows 4 to 6. Purl 3, knit 3.
Size 4. Cast on a multiple of 8.
Rows 1 to 4. Knit 4, purl 4. Rows 5 to 8. Purl 4, knit 4.

No. 5. ROMA.

Both sides of each size are alike, they can be worked in rounds and with an odd number of stitches.
Cast on a multiple of 2.
Size 1. Rows 1 and 2. Knit 1, purl 1. Rows 3 and 4. Purl 1, knit 1.
Size 2. Rows 1 to 3. Knit 1, purl 1. Rows 4 to 6. Purl 1, knit 1.

No. 6. HEMSTITCH.

Every row is the same in each size, so both sides are alike; these do not need extra stitches for the margins.
Size 1. Cast on a multiple of 2.
Row 1. Knit 2, * make 1, knit 2 together, repeat from *.
Size 2. Cast on a multiple of 3.
Row 1. Knit 3, * make 1, knit 2 together, knit 1, repeat from *.
Size 3. Cast on a multiple of 4.
Row 1. Knit 4, * make 1, knit 2 together, knit 2, repeat from *.
Size 4. Cast on a multiple of 5.
Row 1. Knit 5, * make 1, knit 2 together, knit 3, repeat from *.
Size 5. Cast on a multiple of 6.
Row 1. Knit 6, * make 1, knit 2 together, knit 4, repeat from *.

No. 7. PHŒBE.

Cast on a multiple of 2 and 1 more.
Row 1. Knit. Row 2 and every alternate one. Purl. Row 3. Knit 1, * make 1, slip 1, knit 1, over, repeat from *. Finish after row 1. A variation of this can be made by knitting row 2.

No. 8. SPIRA.

Cast on a multiple of 8.
Part 1. Round 1. Knit 1, purl 2, knit 1 and make 1 twice, slip 1, knit 2 together, over. Round 2. Knit.
Part 2. Round 1. Slip 1, knit 2 together, over, make 1 and knit 1 twice, purl 2, knit 1. Round 2. Knit.

No. 9. WAVE.

Cast on a multiple of 8.
Round 1. Purl 1, knit 1, make 1 and knit 1 five times, make 1, purl 1; there will be 14 stitches in each pattern here. Round 2. Purl 2 together, knit 10, purl 2 together. Round 3. Purl 2 together. knit 8, purl 2 together. Round 4. Purl 2 together, knit 6, purl 2 together; there will be 8 stitches in each pattern here.

No. 10. CLERICA.

Cast on a multiple of 8 and 2 more.
Part 1. Row 1. Knit 2, * knit 3, knit 2 together, make 1, knit 3, repeat from *. Row 2 and every alternate one. Knit 2, * purl 6, knit 2, repeat from *. Row 3. Knit 2, * knit 2, knit 2 together, make 1, knit 4, repeat from *. Row 5. Knit 2, * knit 1, knit 2 together, make 1, knit 5, repeat from *. Row 7. Knit 2, * knit 2 together, make 1, knit 6, repeat from *.

Part 2. Row 1. Knit 2, * knit 1, make 1, slip 1, knit 1, over, knit 5, repeat from *. Row 2 and every alternate one. Knit 2, * purl 6, knit 2, repeat from *. Row 3. Knit 2, * knit 2, make 1, slip 1, knit 1, over, knit 4, repeat from *. Row 5. Knit 2, * knit 3, make 1, slip 1, knit 1, over, knit 3, repeat from *. Row 7. Knit 2, * knit 4, make 1, slip 1, knit 1, over, knit 2, repeat from *.

No. 11. BEE.

Cast on a multiple of 4. Knit a row.
Rows 1 to 3. Knit 2, purl 2. Row 4. Knit the second stitch then the first one of each knitted pair, so making them cross, purl 2. Rows 5 to 7. Like Row 1. Row 8. Like row 4. Rows 9 to 11. Purl 2, knit 2. Row 12. Purl 2, cross the knitted pair. Rows 13 to 15. Like row 9. Row 16. Like row 12.

No. 12. DORIC.

Cast on a multiple of 4.
Rounds 1 and 2. Knit 2, purl 2. Round 3. Make 1, purl 2 together. Round 4. Like round 1. Finish after round 2.

No. 13. HOLLINGSCLOUGH.

Cast on a multiple of 4.

Part 1. Row 1. Knit 2, purl 2. Row 2. Purl 1, knit 2, purl 1. Row 3. Purl 2, knit 2. Row 4. Knit 1, purl 2, knit 1.

Part 2. Row 1. Knit 2, purl 2. Row 2. Knit 1, purl 2, knit 1. Row 3. Purl 2, knit 2. Row 4. Purl 1, knit 2, purl 1. Work the same for rounds in each part, which alters the direction of the pattern. This looks very pretty crossed by a welt, 2 rows wide, after every 4, 6 or 8 pattern rows.

No. 14. DIAMOND.

In all the sizes purl row 2 and every alternate one.

Size 1. Cast on a multiple of 4.
Row 1. Make 1, knit 1, make 1, slip 1, knit 2 together, over. Row 3. Slip 1, knit 2 together, over, make 1, knit 1, make 1.

Size 2. Cast on a multiple of 6.
Row 1. Make 1, slip 1, knit 2 together, over, make 1, knit 3. Row 3. Knit 3, make 1, slip 1, knit 2 together, over, make 1.

Size 3. Cast on a multiple of 6.
Row 1. Make 1, knit 1, make 1, slip 1, knit 1, over, knit 1, knit 2 together. Row 3. Make 1, knit 3, make 1, slip 1, knit 2 together, over. Row 5. Slip 1, knit 1, over, knit 1, knit 2 together, make 1, knit 1, make 1. Row 7. Slip 1, knit 2 together, over, make 1, knit 3, make 1.

Size 4. Cast on a multiple of 8.
Row 1. Knit 2, knit 2 together, make 1, knit 1, make 1, slip 1, knit 1, over, knit 1. Row 3. Knit 1, knit 2 together, make 1, knit 3, make 1, slip 1, knit 1, over. Row 5. Knit 2 together, * make 1, knit 5, make 1, slip 1, knit 2 together, over, repeat from *, at the end make 1, knit the last pattern stitch and the first margin one together. Row 7. Knit 1, make 1, slip 1, knit 1, over, knit 3, knit 2 together, make 1. Row 9. Knit 2, make 1, slip 1, knit 1, over, knit 1, knit 2 together, make 1, knit 1. Row 11. Knit 3, make 1, slip 1, knit 2 together, over, make 1, knit 2.

I

Size 5. Cast on a multiple of 10.
Row 1. Knit 3, knit 2 together, make 1, knit 1, make 1, slip 1, knit 1, over, knit 2. Row 3. Knit 2, knit 2 together, make 1, knit 3, make 1, slip 1, knit 1, over, knit 1. Row 5. Knit 1, knit 2 together, make 1, knit 5, make 1, slip 1, knit 1, over. Row 7. Knit 2 together, * make 1, knit 7, make 1, slip 1, knit 2 together, over, repeat from *, at the end make 1, knit the last pattern stitch and the first margin one together. Row 9. Knit 1, make 1, slip 1, knit 1, over, knit 5, knit 2 together, make 1. Row 11. Knit 2, make 1, slip 1, knit 1, over, knit 3, knit 2 together, make 1, knit 1. Row 13. Knit 3, make 1, slip 1, knit 1, over, knit 1, knit 2 together, make 1, knit 2. Row 15. Knit 4, make 1, slip 1, knit 2 together, over, make 1, knit 3.

No. 15. KILT, No. 1.

Size 1. Cast on a multiple of 4.
Part 1. Round 1. Knit 3, purl 1. Round 2. Knit 2, purl 2. Round 3. Knit 1, purl 3. Round 4. Purl.
Part 2. Round 1. Purl 1, knit 3. Round 2. Purl 2, knit 2. Round 3. Purl 3, knit 1. Round 4. Purl.
Size 2. Cast on a multiple of 6.
Part 1. Round 1. Knit 5, purl 1. Round 2. Knit 4, purl 2. Round 3. Knit 3, purl 3. Round 4. Knit 2, purl 4. Round 5. Knit 1, purl 5. Round 6. Purl.
Part 2. Round 1. Purl 1, knit 5. Round 2. Purl 2, knit 4. Round 3. Purl 3, knit 3. Round 4. Purl 4, knit 2. Round 5. Purl 5, knit 1. Round 6. Purl.
Size 3. Cast on a multiple of 8.
Part 1. Round 1. Knit 7, purl 1. Round 2. Knit 6, purl 2. Round 3. Knit 5, purl 3. Round 4. Knit 4, purl 4. Round 5. Knit 3, purl 5. Round 6. Knit 2, purl 6. Round 7. Knit 1, purl 7. Round 8. Purl.
Part 2. Round 1. Purl 1, knit 7. Round 2. Purl 2, knit 6. Round 3. Purl 3, knit 5. Round 4. Purl 4, knit 4. Round 5. Purl 5, knit 3. Round 6. Purl 6, knit 2. Round 7. Purl 7, knit 1. Round 8. Purl.

Size 4. Cast on a multiple of 10.
Part 1. Round 1. Knit 9, purl 1. Round 2. Knit 8, purl 2. Round 3. Knit 7, purl 3. Round 4. Knit 6, purl 4. Round 5. Knit 5, purl 5. Round 6. Knit 4, purl 6. Round 7. Knit 3, purl 7. Round 8. Knit 2, purl 8. Round 9. Knit 1, purl 9. Round 10. Purl.
Part 2. Round 1. Purl 1, knit 9. Round 2. Purl 2, knit 8. Round 3. Purl 3, knit 7. Round 4. Purl 4, knit 6. Round 5. Purl 5, knit 5. Round 6. Purl 6, Knit 4. Round 7. Purl 7, knit 3. Round 8. Purl 8, knit 2. Round 9. Purl 9, knit 1. Round 10. Purl.

No. 16. MELROSE.

Cast on a multiple of 8, and 1 more.
Rows 1, 3, 5 and 7. Purl 1, * knit 2 together, knit 1, make 1 and knit 1 twice, slip 1, knit 1, over, purl 1, repeat from *. Row 2 and every alternate one. Purl. Rows 9, 11, 13 and 15. Knit 1, * make 1, knit 1, slip 1, knit 1, over, purl 1, knit 2 together, knit 1, make 1, knit 1, repeat from *.

When working these designs in rows cast on from 2 to 10 stitches extra for a plain margin at each side, according to the use made of them or their place in a piece of work. Those in 2 parts are the same in each in appearance, though opposite in direction, part 1 rising to the right; both parts should be used for things that have a prominent centre, such as antimacassars, etc., and for articles in pairs, such as babies' boots, etc. Those in 2 or more sizes are the same in construction, though sometimes differing in appearance as they grow larger. Those numbered under one name are alike in construction, but sufficiently varied in appearance to be in this small but useful and easy selection. A pretty variety can be made in some designs by crossing them at regular intervals with welts, 2 or 4 rows wide according to their distance from each other. Many of them also can easily be *transferred from rows to rounds*, work thus: knit instead of purl the second and every alternate round if they are plain ones; if these back rows consist of knitted and purled stitches, reverse them in the rounds, that is, knit the purled ones and purl the knitted ones.

KNEE CAPS.

Two or four needles 10, 1¼ to 3 ozs. of 4 ply Fingering for a pair, 3 ply Fleecy; or needles 11, 3 ply Fingering, 2 ply Fleecy, single Berlin, 4 ply Lady Betty.

The figures refer to No. 3 of the scale.

No. 1. In rows.

Cast on 37 stitches. Knit 8 ridges, but in the sixth row of them after the third stitch, make one and knit two together 3 times to mark the size. Increase in every row after half as many stitches as were cast on, by knitting into the back of the next one and then into the front of it, till there are 63 stitches; this will make a gusset in the middle of the work beginning at its point. Knit 16 ridges without increasing, twice as many as at the beginning; then reduce in every row after half as many stitches as were cast on, by knitting the next two together, till there are as many as were cast on, namely 37. Knit as many ridges as at the beginning, namely 8. Cast off and sew up the seam; or, cast off double with the first row. Use undyed, scarlet or white wool.

No. 2. In rounds.

Cast 24 or 28 stitches on to each of three needles, making a total of 72 or 84. Rib 36 or 40 rounds in twos, then form the gusset thus: work it in plain rows; knit all the stitches on the three needles except the last 2 on the third one; then instead of going on round to the first needle turn and purl back all the stitches except the last 2 on the first needle; continue alternately knitting and purling in rows, leaving in each row the last 2 stitches unknitted or unpurled until all the stitches on the first and third needles are left out of the row, on 12 or 14 levels, and only those on the second or middle needle remain to be worked; slip the first stitch in each of these shortening rows, the last of them will be a purled one and will finish the gusset. These rows can be all knitted, if preferred, so making ridges over the knee. The yarn will now be at the beginning of the middle needle, knit the 24 or 28 stitches on this needle and the same number on the third one, then rib as many *rounds* as at the beginning and cast off loosely.

BABIES' AND DOLLS' BOOTS.

Two needles 11, 4 ply Lady Betty, white and coloured, or ¾ to 1 oz. of single Berlin for sizes 1 to 3; or needles 12, 3 ply Lady Betty, or ½ to ¾ oz. of Andalusian for sizes 2 to 4. For dolls: needles 13, Andalusian; or needles 14, Shetland.

The figures refer to No. 3 of the scales.

The first two of these boots are very simple in their construction, none of them are elaborate; all of them are pretty and can be made quite lovely by the use of fine and good wool, all white or very pale colours, and handsome well contrasted designs in their different parts. A very large variety can be made from these several directions, all essentially different but equally pretty, as a wide choice of designs is given for all the parts, foot, instep, and leg; all of which I used for the 102 pairs of boots I knitted while writing these directions. Some of the designs are simple, others are rather elaborate; these last may sometimes need a little counting of the stitches to fit them into their places, but knitters with only small experience will soon find they can easily accomplish this with most gratifying results. As some designs contract either in their width or length and others expand, it will not do to use both sorts in one boot, for it would put the different parts out of proportion, therefore it will be well to work a small piece of the selected designs with the same needles and wool that are chosen for the boots, to make sure that they are suitable and that they agree or contrast well; it does not look well to use two close or two open designs in one boot, and a close one should always be used for the foot or the shoe; the best ones to begin with in making any of the boots are, for the foot, Huckaback 2, or Roma 1; for the leg, Hemstitch 2, or Phœbe, as they are easy and effective. For a medium sized boot, work size 2 with single Berlin or size 3 with Andalusian. For summer, work one of the three larger sizes with Andalusian and use an open design for the leg; for winter, work one of the three smaller sizes with single Berlin and use a close design for the leg. It is well to use a small wool needle and a piece of white cotton to mark the number of ridges, also, which is rather important, to shew which is the right or outside of the boot; even when working a design this may be needed, as in some of them both sides are alike. Cast off the second way, see contents, as it avoids a chain edge and more nearly resembles the casting on. It will be best to work No. 1 first, both sorts, as they are the simplest, take less wool than the others, and have the fullest directions, most of which are applicable to the rest. Put in a cardboard sole, and a roll of paper in the leg to keep them in shape.

No. 1. THE AMETHYST.

These have a short gusset turned in under the toe; they are very easily and quickly made for they can be worked throughout in plain rows, forming ridges, but are prettier if a close design is used, and still prettier if a close design is used for the foot and an open one for the leg; they can be all white or coloured and white.

1st. Boot. Cast on three stitches with the coloured wool for the gusset, leaving an end to sew up one side of it. Knit three rows, then increase in every other row by knitting into the back and then into the front of the middle stitch till there are 14 stitches, finish with a plain row. Increase in the same way in the first and last stitches in *every* row till there are 40 stitches; in the first of these rows begin the design that is selected for the foot, these are suitable; Huckaback 1 and 2, Roma 1 and 2, * Irene 1, * Ladder, Barbara, see contents in each book; if it can be done begin the design in the last increasing row in the gusset, which will tend to prevent the ridges appearing on the top of the foot. In sizes 1 and 3 an extra row, a back one, will be needed here, without increasing, so as to start the straight rows in the front piece or vamp on the right side of the boot. Work 24 rows with these 40 stitches, without increasing, this is for the vamp; if the design will allow of it slip the first stitch and knit the last in every straight row. In the next row knit 14 stitches for the first side piece, keeping the design right, leave them on the needle or put them on to a piece of cotton, cast off 13 for the instep, that is, one fewer than in the side, leaving one fewer than the right number for the side on the L.H.N. and one on the R.H.N. Work 18 rows with these 14 side stitches for the other side piece. In the next row begin to round the heel thus: knit two together at the outer edge, in this side piece, these will be the last two stitches in the row, work a row without reducing, repeat these two rows till there are eight stitches, five for dolls, then cast off beginning from the outer edge; the design must not be interfered with by the increasings or reducings. Continue the first side piece to match, beginning the row, which will be the second one, at the instep edge. In rounding the heel here the two stitches to be knitted together in every other row at the outer edge, will be the first two in the row; cast off after a plain row, not in the last reducing one, beginning from the outer edge, cut off the wool, unless the boot is all white, leaving an end to sew up the foot. If the foot is knitted in plain rows, forming ridges, there must be two more rows in the vamp and two more in each side piece than are in the scale, because ridges contract the work; the scale for doll's boots is made for ridges. For the leg, begin the white wool and knit up 13 ankle stitches along the inner edge of the side piece just finished, that which has the long end, putting the last into the corner, then 12 across the vamp for the instep, and 13 along the other side piece, making a total of 38 leg stitches. Knit a row back; in the next row knit 2, make 2, knit 2 together; repeat this to the end; for dolls, knit 1, make 1, knit 2 together; this will make ribbon holes round the ankle; knit back treating the new double stitches as single ones. It crushes the ribbon less to make only 4 holes at the back of the ankle, 2 at each end of the row, work thus: knit 2, make 2, knit 2 together, knit 1, make 2, knit 2 together, knit to within 6 stitches of the end, continuing the design correctly, then make 2, knit 2 together, knit 1, make 2, knit 2 together, knit 1. In the next row knit the first 6 stitches and the last 6 plain, continuing the design in the others, a little counting of the stitches may be needed to do this.

For the rest of the leg, work 22 rows in a small close or open design if the foot is in ridges, or use the same close design as in the foot, then cut off the white wool leaving an end to sew up the leg: the designs named before are suitable, also * Willow leaf, * Heene, * Lois, Diamond, Kilt, Hollingsclough, Clerica, Spira, * Colonia, * Clio, * Ionic. Doric, Bee, * Emerald, Wave and Annaberg, see contents in each book; not Brioche and Cable as they contract in width. A pretty leg can be made in several ways, thus: knit 6 or 8 rows in garter work alternately with 6 or 8 in a small open design, such as * Willow leaf, * Lois or Hemstitch; or, knit 6 or 8 rows in stocking work alternately with 6 or 8 in a small open design or the same close one that is used in the foot; or, rib 6 or 8 rows in twos or threes alternately with a few in a small open design or the same close one that is used in the foot, in this case the design must suit the size of the ribs or the effect will not be good; or, work a wide insertion up the front only, such as * Gratia, * Hemstitch 3 or * Wave; or, work 3 or 5 patterns of a narrow insertion up the front only or all round the leg, such as * Balkerne or * Unita; or, work 3, 5 or 7 patterns of a striped design, such as Clerica, in this case and in the previous one the same number of stitches must be put after every repetition of the design and the same number at each end of the row; if an odd number of stitches is needed for the selected design knit up one more in the instep, if two more are needed knit up one in each side. The leg can be worked in rounds after the ribbon holes; for this use any small design that can in any way be transferred from rows to rounds. For the top of the leg, use the coloured wool and knit 8 rows plain, that is, four ridges, this is best if the foot is in ridges; cast off and cut off the wool leaving an end to sew up the top. This top can be made in several ways, thus: rib the number in the scale in twos or threes, according to the design in the leg; or, rib twice the number in the scale and turn it down over the leg, but do not tack it there; or, use the same design as that in the foot, if it is a suitable one, Huckabuck 2 does well for this, especially if it is used all through the boot in coloured and white; or, knit only 2 coloured ridges, then 4 rows in the same design as that used in the leg if it be an open one, in white, then 3 or 4 more coloured ridges, * Lois and Hemstitch do well for this, but not a design with purled stitches in its first row nor one that curves much; or, knit only 1 coloured ridge, and sew on a piece of narrow coloured edging, see book 5; or, sew on a piece of wide coloured edging the wrong side out and turn it down over the leg and tack it there; these last two ways are best for the larger sizes in fine wool. Sew up the seams neatly and not too tightly, the point of the gusset should meet the straight part of the sole, when sewing it draw down the two corners to round the toe a little. Run in the ribbon, ¾ of a yard for a pair, white, or coloured to match the wool; or, sew the ribbon on to the back instead of making holes round the ankle, tie it at opposite sides of the boots and put bows of the same on the toes; or, crochet a white or coloured chain and add tassels or balls, for Andalusian, the chain had better be double, work from two balls at once; the tassels can be mixed white and coloured, wind from two balls at once, 10 times round 2 fingers; if the ankles are tied with a chain a white woollen rosette can be put on to the toe, or, two small tassels or balls united by a chain tied in a bow.

2nd. Sock and shoe. These can be made to imitate socks and shoes, that this may be more apparent use coloured and white wool. Work the coloured shoe by the preceding directions but by the second scale, in which the proportions are for ridges; if a design is used for this shoe, 2 rows must be left out in the vamp and 2 in each side piece, Huckaback 2 and Roma 1 are best for this, and in this case use an open design for the sock. For the instep of the sock, knit up 12 stitches, with the white wool, across the vamp, work 18 rows in a small design, if an odd number of stitches is needed for it, knit up one more stitch and if it contracts in width, work rather loosely or use needles one size larger. The last of these instep rows is a back one; leave the stitches on the needle and cut off

K

the wool leaving an end to sew up both sides, carry it across with a few loose stitches to the second side. For the leg, continue the white wool and knit up 13 ankle stitches along the inner edge of the side piece last finished, that which has the long end, these will extend to the instep, work the instep stitches, continuing the design correctly, and knit up 13 along the other side piece, making a total of 38 leg stitches. Work 28 rows in the leg, the design must continue correctly from the instep and on both sides of it, a little counting of the stitches may be needed to do this, so it is best to begin with a small design, Huckaback 2 if the shoes are in ridges, Hemstitch 1 or 3 if they are worked in a design. For the top, rib 12 rows in ones or twos, to look like a sock. For the *shoe strap*, cast on 4 stitches with the coloured wool; knit 2 rows, knit 2, make 1, knit 2 together, for the button hole, knit plain until it is long enough to encircle the ankle and cast off; sew it on behind and add a pearl button. If the shoe is worked in a design it will be better to work a row of coloured holes round the ankle instead of knitting straps, as they are too narrow to take most designs, except Roma; to do this knit up the ankle stitches with the coloured wool and work as directed for the boots; in this case there will be no need to count the stitches for the design. A welt can be made just before the top ribbing, work thus : knit 1 row, purl 2 rows, knit 2 rows, purl 1 row; in this case leave out 4 rows in the leg.

No. 2. The Beryl.

Both these have a sabot shaped toe which is more apparent if coloured and white wool are used, they can be all white if preferred.

1st Cast on 63 stitches with the coloured wool for twice the length of the sole. Make one by knitting into the back and then into the front of the first stitch, knit to the middle stitch, purl it, knit half the 13 toe stitches, increase as before in the next stitch, finish the row plain. Repeat this increasing row till there are twenty more stitches, namely 83. Knit four rows plain, that is, 2 ridges, purling the middle stitch in every row, it is the one that appears below the level of the rest; cut off the wool leaving an end to sew up the sole. In the next row begin the white wool and reduce for the instep thus: knit to within two stitches of the 13 instep ones, knit two together, knit the 13 instep or middle stitches, after this row always purl the middle one, knit two together, finish the row plain. Repeat this reducing row till there are 39 stitches, purling or knitting all the 13 instep stitches in the back rows; this will form a wide band rising up the instep. In the next row slip 1, then knit 2, make 2, knit 2 together, repeat this to the end for ribbon holes; knit back treating the new double stitches as single ones. For the leg, work 22 rows in a small close or open design; see under Amethyst 1 for this, cut off the wool leaving an end to sew up the leg. For the top of the leg, knit 8 rows plain, with the coloured wool, to match the sole; cast off and cut off the wool leaving an end to sew up the top. Sew up the seams and run in the ribbon. These boots are much prettier if the instep stitches are worked in a small design or a narrow insertion, either of which should be continued all round the leg; if an even number of stitches is needed for this knit the middle stitch and the next one together in the first instep row; if the selected design is a small one the ribbon holes can be made throughout the row, if it is a large one then make two holes only at each end; if the design has purled stitches in its first row begin the pattern with its second row, if this cannot be done knit two instep rows plain, forming a white ridge, reducing twice in each row. Some of the designs and insertions will just fit into some of the sizes, others will need 2 or 3 plain stitches on each side in every row, or, these can be knitted in the front rows and purled in the back ones. Another variation can be made by putting the reducings quite close to the middle stitch, or, by knitting only one stitch plain between the middle stitch and each reducing; this makes the toe rather pointed.

2nd. This is the same as the preceding boot but is worked in the opposite way. Cast on 38 stitches with the

coloured wool for the leg. Knit 8 rows plain. Cut off
the wool leaving an end to sew up the top. With the
white wool work 22 rows in a small close or open design,
see under Amethyst 1 for this, in the last of them knit up
a stitch in the middle, which will be the seam in the instep.
In the next row slip 1, then knit 2, make 2, knit 2 together,
repeat this to the end for the ribbon holes; knit back
treating the new double stitches as single ones. Continue
the white wool and in the next row begin to increase for
the foot thus: knit the 13 ankle stitches, make one by
putting the wool over the needle, knit the 13 instep stitches
purling the seam, make one as before, knit the other 13
ankle stitches. Repeat this increasing row till there are
83 stitches, keeping only 13 instep stitches and adding one
at each side of them in every row; knit the seam stitch in
every back row. All the instep stitches, except the first
and the last, can be purled in every back row; this will
form a knitted rib down each side of the seam on the outside of the boot. The babies' boots can be worked as
follows, which is very pretty, as it forms two ribs on each
side of the seam, each pair of ribs being divided by welts.
Row 1. Knit the ankle stitches, make 1, knit the instep
stitches purling the seam, make 1, knit to the end.
Row 2. Knit the ankle stitches including the new one,
make 1, purl the instep stitches knitting the seam, make 1,
knit to the end beginning with the new one. Row 3.
Knit the ankle stitches including the new one, make 1,
knit 1 or 2, purl 2 or 3, knit 1 or 2, purl the seam, work
the other half of the instep like the first one, make 1, knit
to the end beginning with the new one. Row 4. Knit
the ankle stitches including the new one, make 1, purl 1
or 2, knit 2 or 3, purl 1 or 2, knit the seam, work the
other half of the instep like the first one, make 1, knit to
the end beginning with the new one. Repeat these 4
increasing rows till there is the right number of stitches.
Another variation can be made by putting the increasings
quite close to the middle stitch, or, by knitting only one
stitch plain between the middle stitch and each increasing;
this makes the toe rather pointed. Cut off the white wool

leaving an end to sow up the leg. For the sole, knit four
rows plain, that is, 2 ridges, with the coloured wool, to
match the top, purling the seam stitch in every row after
the first one. In the next row reduce thus: slip one, knit
two together, knit to the seam stitch, purl it, knit half the
instep stitches, knit two together, knit plain to the end.
Repeat this reducing row till there are 63 stitches. Turn
the boot inside out and cast off double, beginning from
the heel, knit four together at the beginning of the row
and three together at the end of it. Sew up the seams
and run in the ribbon.

No. 3. THE CHRYSOLYTE.

These have the toe gathered into a small circle sewn in
underneath, they can be all white or coloured and white.

1st. Boot. In 3 sizes, matching 2, 3 and 4 in the scales;
needles 12, and Andalusian are needed. Cast on 22, 24
or 26 stitches with the coloured wool for the length of the
sole, leaving an end to gather the toe and sew in the circle.
In the first row knit 3, make 1 in the next stitch by
knitting into the back and then into the front of it, knit
to the end, increasing, as before, in the last stitch, which
is the heel end of the row; knit a row plain. Repeat
these 2 rows till there are 10 more stitches, namely 32, 34
or 36, the last row being a plain one. Continue increasing
as before, but at the toe only, till there are 38, 40 or 42
stitches, still knitting a plain row after every increasing
one; this will bring the wool to the toe; then knit 2, 4 or
6 rows plain, that is, 1, 2 or 3 ridges; in the last of these
plain rows cast off 14, 15 or 16, beginning from the heel,
leaving 24, 25 or 26 at the toe and 1 on the R.H.N. Knit
these 25, 26 or 27 vamp stitches, this will form the last
ridge in the side, continue knitting them till there are 10,
11 or 12 short ridges for the instep or vamp; this will bring
the wool to the toe. Knit the vamp stitches and cast on to
the same needle 13, 14 or 15 stitches, rather loosely to match
the casting off at the other side, making the same number
as before casting off, namely 38, 40 or 42. Knit back
plain; this will bring the wool to the toe; then knit 2

fewer plain rows than there are on the other side, because the casting on and the return back row make a ridge; this will bring the wool to the toe. In the next row knit 3, knit 2 together, finish the row plain; knit a row plain. Repeat these 2 rows till there are as many stitches at the top of the heel as there are on the other side, namely, 32, 34 or 36. Continue reducing in the same way at the toe, and round the heel on this side by knitting together the last 2 stitches in the same row, still knitting a plain row after every reducing one, till there are as many stitches as were first cast on, namely, 22, 24 or 26. Cast off after finishing the last plain row, beginning from the toe, and cut off the wool leaving an end to sew up the heel. A very pretty vamp can be made thus : knit only 1 ridge; work 6 or 8 rows in Huckaback 2, Roma 1, * Lois or Hemstitch 2; then 4 or 5 ridges ; 6 or 8 more pattern rows; and 1 more ridge ; this will bring the wool to the toe; continue as before ; or, work 10 or 12 rows in Hollingsclough or * Heene 1, part 1 of either, then the same number of rows in part 2, or work part 2 first. If a close design is used in the vamp, work the same for the top and use an open one for the leg; if an open design is used for the vamp, work the same for the leg and knit ridges for the top. If these boots are being made with white and coloured wool, it looks exceedingly well to work these 2 pattern spaces in the vamp with the white wool, *all* the rest of the foot and the top being coloured ridges ; an open design is best for this, Hemstitch 2 and * Lois are suitable, use the same for the leg, which should be white also. For the leg, with the white wool knit up 12, 13 or 14 ankle stitches along the inner edge of the side piece just finished, then 10, 12 or 14 across the vamp for the instep, and 12, 13 or 14 along the other side piece, making a total of 34, 38 or 42 leg stitches. Knit a row back; make the ribbon holes; knit a row back. Work 20, 22 or 24 leg rows in a small repeating design; knit 6, 8 or 10 coloured rows plain, that is, 3, 4 or 5 ridges, and cast off. Gather the toe and sew up the seams, then for the circle work thus : cast on 3 stitches, increase in the first stitch in every row till the piece is wide enough for its place, then knit together the first 2 stitches in every row till there are 3, and cast off; sew it in and add the ribbon. See under Amethyst 1 for fuller directions.

2nd. Sock and shoe. In 3 sizes, matching 2, 3 and 4 in the scales. These can be made to imitate socks and shoes, that this may be more apparent use coloured and white wool; needles 13 and Andalusian are needed. Work the coloured shoe in the same way as the boot, all in plain knitting producing ridges. Cast on 28, 30 or 32; increase to 38, 40 or 42; then increase further to 44, 46 or 48; knit 1, 2 or 3 plain ridges; cast off 32, 33 or 34, leaving 13, 14 or 15 vamp stitches; knit 15 16 or 17 vamp ridges; cast on 31, 32 or 33, making a total of 44, 46 or 48; knit the plain ridges; reduce to 38, 40 or 42; then reduce further to 28, 30 or 32 and cast off. Continue the coloured wool and work a welt round the top of the shoe, thus: knit up along the edge of the side piece just finished as many stitches as were there cast off, then 14, 16 or 18 across the vamp for the instep, and the same number as before along the other side piece, making a total of 78, 82 or 86 welt stitches; knit back, purl a row, knit back. Cut off the wool leaving an end to sew up the heel and sole. Put all the stitches at both sides on to a piece of cotton, work the instep stitches for 18, 20 or 22 rows in a small open repeating design, Phœbe and * Lois are easy to begin with, see contents in each book. Cut off the wool leaving an end to sew up the sides of the instep. With the outside of the shoe to you put the first 15, 16 or 17 side stitches, which are for the ankle, on to a needle, slip the instep stitches on to the same needle, and put the last 15, 16 or 17 other side stitches, which are for the other ankle, on to it also, making a total of 44, 48 or 52 leg stitches. Continue the white wool for the leg and work 32, 34 or 36 rows in the sock design, which must continue correctly from the last instep row and on each side of it. Rib 12, 14 or 16 rows in ones or twos and cast off leaving an end to sew up the leg. For the shoe straps and for fuller directions see under Amethyst 2. Sew up the seams, also the stitches left at each side of the instep to the edge of the sock. These look very lace like and pretty if the socks are worked in Shetland wool, for this put 2 or 4 more stitches in the instep and the leg and work 2 or 4 more rows in each part of the sock.

PENCE JUG.

Four needles 14, ½ oz. of 4 ply Fingering; or needles 15, ¼ oz. of single Berlin.

Cast on 3 stitches leaving an end 4 inches long. Work 2½ inches for the handle in Brioche, see contents, in the last row omit the made stitch, leaving 2. Cast 12 stitches on to this needle, 15 on to the second, the 11 middle ones of which are for the lip, and 12 on to the third. Rib in twos, except the 11 middle stitches, on each side of which there will be a furrow. The 2 under the handle are to be knitted, and will always be the first in the round. Work the lip thus: knit the 11 stitches plain in the first 3 rounds; in the next round knit 1, purl 2 together, knit plain to within the last 3 of the lip, purl 2 together, knit 1; knit the 9 lip stitches plain in the next round, ribbing the rest. Repeat these 2 rounds till there are 5 lip stitches, then knit 1, purl 3 together, knit 1, in the next round knit these 3 stitches, and in the following one knit 1, knit 2 together. Continue knitting these 2 stitches which will form the opposite rib to the one under the handle; equalise the number of stitches on the needles as the lip decreases. The number of stitches now will be 32. Rib in twos for 6 rounds after the lip. Knit 3 rounds, purl 3 rounds, knit 1 round, make 1 and knit 2 all round, knit 1 round. The number of stitches now will be 48. * Purl 3 rounds, knit 1 round, make 1 and knit 2 together all round, knit 1 round; repeat from *. Purl 3 rounds, knit 1 round, knit 2 together and knit 2 all round, knit 1 round. The number of stitches now will be 36. Purl 3 rounds, knit 1 round, knit 2 together and knit 2 all round till there are 9 stitches, put the wool through them and fasten off. Sew the end of the handle on to the neck leaving a small knob. This jug is much prettier worked in two colours, or in two or three shades of one colour; it is useful for Christmas trees filled with coins, buttons, hooks, etc.

TAM O' SHANTERS.

Four needles 10, 2½ ozs. of double Berlin for size 1 ; or needles 11, 1½ or 2 ozs. of 4 ply Fingering for sizes 1 and 2 ; or needles 12, 1¼ oz. of single Berlin for size 3. For dolls, needles 13, Andalusian ; or needles 14, Shetland.

Cast 3 stitches on to each of the first two needles and 2 on to the third, making a total of 8. Make all the new stitches by crossing the yarn over the needle. Round 1. Make 1, knit 1, repeat 7 times in this and in every increasing round, making 8 divisions in the circle. Round 2, and every alternate one. Knit. Round 3. Make 1, knit 2. Round 5. Make 1, knit 3. Continue increasing thus in every other round till there are 20, 22 or 24 stitches in every division, making a total of 160, 176 or 192. Finish with a plain round. This will make a flat circle. Purl 2 rounds ; then reduce thus : knit 2 together, knit 18, 20 or 22, repeat 7 times in this and in every reducing round, keeping 8 divisions in the circle. Knit a round plain. Continue reducing thus in every other round, knitting one stitch fewer in every division, till there are 14, 16 or 18 in each one, making a total of 112, 128 or 144. Finish with a plain round. In the next round make the ribbon holes thus : knit 2, make 2, knit 2 together twice, repeat to the end; this will also reduce the stitches for the band to 94, 107 or 120. Knit a round plain, treating the new double stitches as single ones. If there is an odd number here knit 2 together at the end of the round. Rib 10, 12 or 14 rounds in twos tightly and cast off. If there are 2 stitches over in the first of these ribbed rounds put one into each of the last two furrows. If the band is needed tighter work it with needles one size smaller than those used for the rest of the cap. Put a short thick tassel of the same yarn in the middle of the top and run in ¾ of a yard of narrow ribbon. It takes 4 ozs. of double Berlin to make size 3, which will fit a large man or woman. For dolls, increase to 9, 11 or 13 in every division, making a total of 72. 88 or 104 ; purl 2 rounds ; reduce to 6, 8 or 10 in every division, making a total of 48, 64 or 80 ; make the ribbon holes, reducing again to 41, 54 or 67 ; rib 6, 7 or 8 rounds in ones.

L

THE DIVIDED GUSSET KNEE.

This can be applied to any stocking, but is useful chiefly for cyclists and children: the gusset more especially for the bent knees of the former; the division for children, as their stockings wear out much faster at the knee than elsewhere in the leg, and this knee can be taken out and a new one put in, also the part over the knee can be strengthened by adding a finer yarn, as directed for the heel and toe, see page 13. It is worked in rows; slip the first stitch and knit the last in every row in each part. The size following is No. 3 of the scale. Cast on to one needle 10 stitches fewer than half of the total number in the scale, that will be 35; this is to place the side seams a little to the back of the leg, it includes the seam stitch, which will be the middle one in the row, there being an odd number; leave an end here to sew up one side. Rib 30 rows for the top or make a hem; then alternately knit and purl in rows, to produce stocking work, as many as will reach to just above the calf; the number of rows cannot be given as that depends on the length of leg needed, if for a tall or short person, but this division should extend far enough to allow of all the worn out part at the knee being removed. Mark the size in the right place and make the seam in the leg by purling the middle stitch in every knitted or front row; the last of these rows will be a knitted one. On to this needle cast as many more stitches as are needed to make up the total number in the scale, namely 54; arrange the 89 stitches on to three needles according to the scale, putting the seam stitch at the end of the third needle; make the circle and with the fourth needle work in *rounds*, finishing the stocking as before directed, see page 12. For the knee work upwards to the top ribbing thus: knit up, across the half way edge, as many stitches as were there cast on, namely 54; if the new stitches are made into the loops that fall forward, over the right side, the join will scarcely appear; purl back, * then alternately knit and purl as many plain rows as will reach to just below the knee, and form the gusset thus: continue knitting and purling plain, but in every row leave the last 2 stitches unknitted or unpurled on the L.H.N.; do this till there are about half of the 54 stitches left in the middle in a short row, that will be 26, and a quarter, namely 14, left at each side, on 7 levels; slip the first stitch in each of these shortening rows, the last of them will be a purled one, and will finish the gusset. In the next row knit the 26 middle stitches and the following 14 side ones; turn and purl all these 40 stitches and the other 14 side ones, making 54 in all. If the knee is needed more bent leave only one stitch on the L.H.N. each time of turning. * Continue alternately knitting and purling, with the 54 stitches, as many plain rows as are needed to make the upper part as long as the under part; rib the top as before or make the hem, which must be felled down after being finished. Cast off leaving an end to sew up one side. Sew up the seams and darn in the ends. To renew this knee, undo the seams, cut off the sound part at the top, remove the worn out part, unravel a few rows, knit up the stitches and work from * to *. If the gusset is not needed leave out all between the asterisks.

SHIELDS.

Two pins 9, 3½ ozs. of Alloa.

Cast on 74 stitches. Slip the first stitch and knit the last in every row. Rib 48 rows in twos, about 8 inches. In the next row cast off 9, leaving 65 on the L.H.N., rib these; in the following row again cast off 9, leaving 57 on the L.H.N. and 1 on the R.H.N., rib these, and continue ribbing the 58 stitches for 8 rows. In the next row knit 2, knit 2 together, knit plain to the end; repeat this reducing row till there are 48 stitches, that will be 5 ridges, then knit plain for 76 rows, that will be 38 ridges. Reduce, as before, to 28, making 53 ridges in all and cast off. This flap for the chest will be about 13 inches long. Sew up the sides of the ribbing to make a collar for the throat and fold it down in half. A row of double crochet, very loosely worked, round all the ribbed edges is a great protection to them.

UHLAN CAPS.

Four needles 8, 4½ ozs. of Alloa.

Cast 3 stitches on to each of three needles, making a total of 9. Round 1. Make 1, knit 1 to the end. Round 2. Knit. Round 3. Make 1, knit 2, make 1, knit 1, repeat 5 times in this and in each increasing round, making 6 divisions in the circle. Rounds 4 to 6. Knit. Round 7. Make 1, knit 4, make 1, knit 1. Rounds 8 to 10. Knit. Round 11. Make 1, knit 6, make 1, knit 1. Rounds 12 to 14. Knit. Round 15. Make 1, knit 8, make 1, knit 1. Rounds 16 to 18. Knit. Round 19. Make 1, knit 10, make 1, knit 1. Rounds 20 to 22. Knit. Round 23. Make 1, knit 12, make 1, knit 1. Rounds 24 to 26. Knit. Round 27. Make 1, knit 15. There will be 96 stitches here. Rib 14 rounds in twos, this head piece should be about 6 inches long. On the first needle knit 2, put these back on to the third needle, this is to bring a *rib* at each side of the face, cast off 30. Continue ribbing the 66 stitches in twos for 9 *rows*, about an inch. Cast on 30, replace the 2 stitches on to the first needle and continue ribbing the 96 stitches for 100 *rounds*, making the cap 22 inches long in all. Cast off very loosely. Work a row of double crochet round the opening for the face and round the bottom edge, both quite loosely.

STRIPED INVERTED TOP FOR HOSE.

This is a handsome addition to men's hose for shooting, etc., as the stripes round the top are very striking. Use two colours that contrast well, navy and red, or those of the Club, etc., to which the recipient of the hose belongs. Cast on with the navy and work as before directed, see page 11 ; if the hose is to be ribbed throughout or worked in a design, make a hem ; if it is to be plain, rib from 12 to 20 rounds in twos. All the striped part is to be knitted plain. Knit from 2 to 6 rounds ; then begin the red and knit a broad stripe, follow it by a narrow one of navy, before beginning another colour *knit* the seam stitch with both colours ; there should be an odd number of red stripes and they should be wider than the space that divides them; they look well in different widths, the narrowest being at the top, when in wear, or otherwise prettily arranged. When the stripes are done cut off the red yarn and use the navy for the rest of the hose; with it knit from 20 to 30 rounds plain, then turn this striped piece inside out, put the seam stitch back on to what was the first needle and which will be henceforth the third one, and rib in twos a piece as long as from the first to the last red rounds; the first of these ribbed rounds will be worked back over the previous plain one, that is, in beginning the ribbing, work those stitches that are on the needle that has just been filled and continue round, so changing the first and third needles. The striped piece will be folded down over this ribbing which should not shew at either end.

GRAFTING.

To graft is to unite the edges of two pieces of plain stocking knitting or of woven webbing in such a way that the join cannot be seen; it is worked from right to left, on the right side of the article; use a wool needle and the same yarn of which the article is made. Work thus: unravel the stitches of both edges till they are all on the same level and quite straight and clear, place them flat and close to each other, so that the head of each loop fits into the space between two loops on the opposite side; darn in the end of the yarn firmly, then put the needle down into the first loop on the right hand side, whether on the upper or lower edge, up through the next loop on the same edge, down through the loop on the opposite edge that occupies the space between the two previous ones, up through its next one; so piercing two loops on one edge, down and up, and two loops on the other edge, down and up, the latter pair beginning half a loop after the former pair; then put the needle down into the second loop of the first pair and repeat till the join is finished: each loop is pierced twice, once down and once up; two are pierced at one stitch, namely, a pair of loops on one side and a pair on the other alternately.

CUFFS.
No. 8. WELTED EDGE.

All the sizes, whether ribbed in 2, 3 or 4, or worked in a design, can be edged at the hand end with 2 or 3 welts of the same or of another colour, work thus: rib the length in the scale in black or in any dark colour, then do not cut off the yarn, but with a light colour, say * red, knit 1 round, purl 3 rounds, then purl 2 and make 1 and purl 2 together all round, purl 3 rounds; with black, knit 4 rounds; repeat from *, then work another red welt as before and cast off the first way.

HOODS.
No. 3. TRIANGLE.

Two pins 5. $2\frac{1}{3}$, 3 or $3\frac{1}{2}$ ozs. of 4 ply Fingering; or pins 6, single Berlin, $2\frac{3}{4}$ ozs. for size 1. For dolls, needles 10, Andalusian; or needles 11, Shetland.

Cast on 86, 98 or 110 stitches. Slip the first stitch and knit the last in every row. Work 118, 134 or 150 rows in Roma 1, Huckaback 2, or any small, close repeating design that has 2, 3 or 4 stitches in a pattern, not Brioche, * Clio, nor any design that forms a rib, see contents in each book; this should be a square about 20, 22 or 24 inches in Fingering. Cast off and fold it to make a double triangle. Crochet a row of scallops along both the shorter sides, working through both edges so as to close up the triangle. Put a large box pleat, stitched about an inch from the edge, in the middle of the long crossway side, or, use the yarn double and gather up about the same length, this is for the top of the head. For the neck gather up the triangle across the three corners, curving down a little into the middle or right angle to give room for the head, this corner will hang down the back and the two acute angles down the chest; put most of the gathers at each side, between the corners, that is, over the ears, where they should be about an inch from the edge of the knitting. Put a rosette or tuft of the same yarn at the top and add crochet strings with a tassel to each; or, put a few bows of ribbon at the top and strings to match. For dolls, cast on 38 or 50 stitches and work 60 or 80 rows.

SEAMEN'S KNITTING.

The following articles will be most acceptable to The Missions to Seamen; 11, Buckingham Street, Strand, London, W.C.; addressed to the Secretary, who has approved of the specimens I knitted and and sent to him. Any colour will do, in rather dark shades. Cuffs cover the wrist only; mittens cover the wrist and the hand and thumb as far as the first knuckle of the former; hand mufflers, or Canadian gloves, cover the wrist and the whole hand, the four fingers being in one compartment; all these are made with the same needles and yarn and number of stitches cast on. Tight knitters had better use needles one size larger in each case.

Comforters. Two pins 7, 11 ozs. of Alloa. Cast on size 2 of the scale, knit plain for 2 yards; or, work a small design, Huckaback, Roma, etc., see contents, not Brioche nor * Clio, as they are ribs and contract the work in its width; see page 45. *Cuffs.* Four needles 12, 1¼ oz. of Alloa. Cast on size 4 of the scale, rib in 1, 2, 3 or 4; see page 43. *Mittens.* Four needles 12, 2¼ ozs. of Alloa. Cast on size 2 of the scale, work 10 rounds fewer in the wrist and rib in 1 round the hand and thumb; see page 38. *Shields.* See page 75. *Steering Gloves.* Four needles 12, 3 ozs. of Alloa. These are made like Hand Mufflers and Babies' Gloves 2. Cast on size 4 of the scale for the latter. see pages 47 and 36. For *very strong ones* use needles 11, 7 ozs. of Fisherman's yarn, grey or unbleached. Cast on size 1 of the scale, knit only 10 more plain rounds in the hand and only 8 more in the thumb than the number in the scale; they should be about 13 inches long and 6 across the hand and thumb *Sea boot stockings.* Four needles 10, 20 ozs. of Fisherman's yarn. Cast on and work size 0 of the scale; see page 11, with these alterations ; 12 rounds ribbed, 54 before reducing, 11 leg reductions, 5 plain between them, making 61 calf rounds, leaving 43 stitches, 18 ankle rounds, 22 instep stitches, 21 heel stitches, 49 before reducing, 3 ankle reductions, leaving 43 stitches, 28 plain foot rounds, 8 toe reductions. The leg will be about 26 inches long and the foot about 11 inches. *Uhlan cap.* See page 76.

CLOCKS OR CLOX.

These are ornamental lines, headed by a device, at each ankle in the stocking; they can be worked, in plain hose only, by purling alternate stitches in every other round. The size following is No. 3 of the scale. Begin the device when half the leg reducings are done and work thus: halve the total number of stitches cast on, that will be 44, so the forty-fourth stitches from the seam will be the 2 middle ones in the front of the stocking, mark between them with a piece of cotton; then halve the heel stitches, that will be 16, so the sixteenth stitch on each side of the cotton will be the one to be purled as the top middle one in the device at each ankle; starting from this point will make the line end where the heel is divided. A diamond is easy to begin with, so in the third clock round, purl the stitch on each side of the top middle one; in the fifth, purl one outside each of these two and the middle one also; in the seventh, purl 4; in the ninth, purl 5; and so on until the device is wide enough according to the size of the hose and the sort of yarn that is being used. Reduce the diamond in the same gradation till there are from 2 to 5 purled stitches. Continue purling these stitches in alternate rounds to form the line, till the heel is divided. The leg reducings must be made in the right places and a plain round knitted after every pattern round. An initial can be used for the device, and the line can be varied according to taste, thus: purl 1; in the next pattern round, purl 2; in the next, purl 3; repeat this, so making a column of small triangles.

Knitters who like to *ornament the top* of plain hose can work from 6 to 12 or more rounds of a close or open design after the hem or the top ribbing is finished; knit 3 or 4 plain rounds first and choose a design that has 2, 4 or 8 stitches in a pattern, Spira and Hollingsclough are suitable, see contents: in a large family a different design or colour can be used for each person, so that each can readily recognize her own hose. A *furrow* at each side of the *heel flap* is an improvement, work thus: purl the second and fourth stitches from each end of each front row, knitting the intermediate ones. For braces and garters use a design or an insertion that is alike or equally pretty on both sides. Any of the babies' boots make good sleeping socks for children, use the needles and yarns given on page 48; the toe stitches of the Beryl boots can be gathered to a point instead of being cast off. For *dolls' bootakins* use needles 13, Andalusian; or needles 14, Shetland; the scale is for Beryl 1st, size 3, and for Amethyst 1st, size 3. The *wrists* of *babies' gloves*, of both sorts, can be made very pretty by using * Clio, which can be worked in rounds thus: 4 stitches in a pattern. Round 1. Knit 1, purl 3. Round 2. Knit 2, purl 1, knit 1. They can also be made in Brioche, for this cast on to one needle about two thirds more stitches than the number in the scale for the size that is to be worked, e.g. for size 3 cast on 74, which will allow for a plain stitch at each end of the row; work the right length in rows; in the next row * knit 1, knit 2 together, repeat from *, then in the following row knit 2 together at regular intervals to reduce the stitches to the right number in the scale; this will make a cuff or gauntlet large enough to cover a child's long sleeve and so add greatly to the warmth. The gusset in *knee cap* 1 can be begun broad instead of pointed by increasing in the second or third stitch from the middle one of the number cast on; decrease for the second gusset at the same distance from the edge, this will make the kneecap less bent. Vest No. 3 can be *ornamented* with a close repeating design over the *chest*; choose one that has 2 or 4 stitches in a pattern and begin to work it when about two thirds of the plain ridges are done, knit one third of the stitches plain at each end of each row. In the frill for cuffs pinch the middle of each rib on the right side to make it lie evenly; it is a great improvement to work a round of *ribbon holes* about an inch before beginning the frill, 1 yard of ribbon is enough for a pair. Cuffs look well worked in 3 bands of ribbing divided by 2 of a suitable design, one that fits the size of the ribs; another pretty variety, the *sexagon cuff*, can be made by working half of the stitches on *each* needle in a design, the

M

other half being ribbed, this part must begin and end with a rib, not a furrow; the following look well, rib in ones and work Roma 1, or, rib in twos and work Huckaback 2. The designs in 2 or more sizes and in 2 parts are most useful for an article in which the same pattern is needed for its several parts but in different sizes, and for one in which the direction of the design should slant in opposite ways, such as a frock or spencer. I am often asked what size in the hose *scale* matches a *shop* sock or stocking that will fit a medium sized man; this question cannot be answered satisfactorily owing to the variation of knitters which causes a difference of 2 or 3 sizes in the same article and affects also the quantity of yarn used, sometimes to the extent of an ounce or more in a small piece of work; this may make the weights I give appear insufficient, but they are all from my own working and I knit neither tightly nor loosely but just closely; sizes 2 or 3 made with needles 13 and 4 ply Fingering will be almost sure to answer the purpose, but the following suggestions may help to ensure a certainty which can be best gained by experience; rib an inch in twos, then knit 2 inches plain and cast off, this can be kept as a guide, lay it on a sock that fits the intended wearer and if both stretch to the same width when equally pulled on the first two fingers of each hand, then the knitted sock will fit. The first half, or more, of this book was taken through the press when I was nursing my father, the late Vicar of Castleton, in his last long illness, this will account for the division of some of the subjects, and for any error; I had not then time to work the articles, they have been done since. Thanks to the printer there is no need to turn a page while working an article, unless the length of the subject demands it, which occurs only a very few times. See books 2 and 3 for more repeating designs, etc.

THE WARLEIGH SCALE FOR BOOTS.

No. 1. THE AMETHYST.

	1st.	Dolls.			Babies.		
Size	1	2	3	1	2	3	4
Increase to	7	8	9	12	13	14	15
Increase to	19	22	25	34	37	40	43
Vamp rows	14	16	18	20	22	24	26
Side stitches	7	8	9	12	13	14	15
Stitches cast off ..	6	7	8	11	12	13	14
Side rows	10	12	14	14	16	18	20
Ankle stitches	8	9	10	11	12	13	14
Instep stitches	4	6	8	8	10	12	14
Total leg stitches.	20	24	28	30	34	38	42
Leg rows	8	10	12	18	20	22	24
Top rows	2	4	6	4	6	8	10

See page 62.

THE WARLEIGH SCALE FOR BOOTS.
No. 1. THE AMETHYST.

2nd.	Dolls.		Babies.			
Size	1	2	1	2	3	4
Increase to	8	9	12	13	14	15
Increase to	22	25	34	37	40	43
Vamp rows	2	2	2	4	6	8
Side stitches	8	9	12	13	14	15
Stitches cast off	7	8	11	12	13	14
Side rows	28	30	32	34	36	38
Instep stitches	7	8	8	10	12	14
Sock instep rows	8	10	14	16	18	20
Ankle stitches	9	10	11	12	13	14
Total leg stitches	25	28	30	34	38	42
Leg rows	18	20	24	26	28	30
Top rows	6	6	8	10	12	14

See page 65.

THE WARLEIGH SCALE FOR BOOTS.
No. 2. THE BERYL.

1st.

	Dolls.				Babies.			
Size	1	2	3	4	1	2	3	4
Stitches cast on ..	27	31	35	39	47	55	63	71
Toe stitches	1	3	5	7	9	11	13	15
Increase to	35	39	47	55	67	75	83	91
Ridges	0	1	2	3	0	1	2	3
Instep stitches	1	3	5	7	9	11	13	15
Reduce to	15	19	23	27	31	35	39	43
Leg rows	6	8	10	12	18	20	22	24
Top rows	4	4	6	6	4	6	8	10

See page 66.

THE WARLEIGH SCALE FOR CHEST WRAPS.

Size	1	2	3	4	5	6
Stitches cast on	13	19	25	31	37	43
Ridges	4	5	6	7	8	9
Increase to	85	95	105	115	125	135
Ridges	12	13	14	15	16	17
Shoulder stitches	30	34	38	42	46	50
Ridges	46	48	50	52	54	56
Ozs. in 4 ply Fingering ..	2¼	3¼	3¾	4½	5¼	3⅓

See page 30.

THE WARLEIGH SCALE FOR BOOTS.
No. 2. THE BERYL.

2nd.   Dolls.   Babies.

Size	1	2	3	4	1	2	3	4
Stitches cast on	14	18	22	26	30	34	38	42
Top rows	4	4	6	6	4	6	8	10
Leg rows	6	8	10	12	18	20	22	24
Ankle stitches	7	8	9	10	11	12	13	14
Instep stitches	1	3	5	7	9	11	13	15
Increase to	35	39	47	55	67	75	83	91
Ridges	0	1	2	3	0	1	2	3
Reduce to	27	31	35	39	47	55	63	71

See page 67.

THE WARLEIGH SCALE FOR BOOTAKINS.
No. 2.

Dolls.   Babies.

Size	1	2	1	2	3	4
Total leg stitches	22	28	30	34	38	42
Ankle rows	16	18	22	24	26	28
Increase to	32	38	40	44	48	52
Calf ridges	14	16	18	22	26	30
Side stitches	8	10	11	12	13	14
Middle stitches	16	18	18	20	22	24
Thigh ridges	5	6	8	9	10	11
Rows ribbed in twos	6	8	10	12	14	16

See page 50.

THE WARLEIGH SCALE FOR BABIES' GLOVES

Nos. 1 and 2.						
Size	1	2	3	4	5	6
Stitches cast on	12	14	14	16	18	18
	12	14	14	16	18	18
	12	12	16	16	16	20
Total	36	40	44	48	52	56
Wrist rounds ribbed	22	24	26	28	30	32
No. 1, continued.						
Pattern rounds..........	36	40	44	48	52	56
Number of stitches	12	8	12	8	12	8
No. 2, continued.						
Plain rounds............	6	6	9	9	12	12
Thumb stitches	12	14	16	18	20	22
Thumb rounds..........	18	21	24	27	30	33
Number of stitches	48	54	60	66	72	78
Gusset stitches..........	6	6	6	8	8	8
Plain rounds............	12	14	16	18	20	22
Reducing rounds	4	4	5	5	6	6
Number of stitches	20	24	24	28	28	32
Thumb rounds..........	8	10	12	14	16	18

See page 36.

THE WARLEIGH SCALE FOR COMFORTERS.

Size	1	2	3	4	5	6
Stitches cast on ..	38	50	62	74	86	98
Marginal ridges ..	150	160	170	180	190	200

See page 45.

THE WARLEIGH SCALE FOR LEGGINGS.

Size	1	2	3	4	5	6
	18	22	24	28	30	34
Stitches cast on	18	22	24	28	30	34
	20	20	24	24	28	28
Total	56	64	72	80	88	96
Top rounds ribbed	20	20	20	20	20	20
Plain leg rounds	52	56	60	64	68	72
Leg reducing rounds	7	8	9	10	11	12
Calf rounds	37	43	49	55	61	67
Number of stitches	42	48	54	60	66	72
Plain ankle rounds	8	12	16	20	24	28
Ankle rounds ribbed	20	20	20	20	20	20
Ozs. in 4 ply Fingering..		3	$3\frac{1}{4}$	$3\frac{3}{4}$	$4\frac{1}{2}$	$5\frac{1}{2}$

See page 39.

THE WARLEIGH SCALE FOR KNEE CAPS.

Size	1	2	3	4	5	6	7	8
Stitches cast on	29	33	37	41	45	49	53	57
Ridges	6	7	8	9	10	11	12	13
Increase to	51	57	63	69	75	81	87	93
Ridges	12	14	16	18	20	22	24	26

See page 60.

THE WARLEIGH SCALE FOR STAYS.

	Dolls			Children.				
Size	1	2	3	1	2	3	4	5	6
Stitches cast on	18	24	30	43	54	60	66	72	78
Back rows	28	32	36	84	88	92	96	100	104
Stitches cast off	4	6	8	10	12	14	16	18	20
Stitches left on	14	18	22	38	42	46	50	54	58
Arm rows	6	8	10	14	16	18	20	22	24
Gusset stitches	6	8	10	10	12	14	16	18	20
Front rows	44	48	52	144	148	152	156	160	164
Strap stitches	3	4	5	5	6	7	8	9	10
Strap rows	24	28	32	44	48	52	56	60	64

See page 49.

THE WARLEIGH SCALE FOR VESTS. No. 1.

Size	D	1	2	3	4	5	6	7	8	9	10
Stitches cast on	21	41	49	57	65	73	81	89	97	106	113
Rows ribbed in ones	37	48	60	72	84	96	108	120	132	144	156
Shoulder strap stitches	11	14	17	20	23	26	29	32	35	38	41
Shoulder strap rows	8	8	8	12	12	16	16	20	20	24	24
Gusset stitches	16	11	12	13	14	15	16	17	18	19	20

See page 34.

THE WARLEIGH SCALE FOR VESTS. No. 2.

Size	D	1	2	3	4	5	6	7	8	9	10
Stitches cast on	26	42	50	58	66	74	82	90	98	106	114
Rows ribbed in twos	4	6	6	6	8	8	8	8	10	10	10
Plain rows	12	20	22	24	26	28	30	32	34	36	38
Rows ribbed in twos	34	50	60	70	80	90	100	110	120	130	140
Shoulder stitches	6	10	10	12	12	14	14	16	16	18	18
Stitches cast off	14	22	30	34	42	46	54	58	66	70	78
Shoulder strap rows	8	12	14	16	18	20	22	24	26	28	30
Sleeve stitches	6	8	8	10	10	12	12	14	14	16	16
Sleeve rows	42	60	72	84	93	108	120	132	144	156	168
Ozs. in 4-ply Fingering.		2½	3½	4	5	6¼	7¼	8¼	10¼	1¼	4¼

See page 34.

THE WARLEIGH SCALE FOR VESTS. No. 3.

Size	D	1	2	3	4	5	6	7	8	9	10
Stitches cast on	31	42	50	58	66	74	82	90	98	106	114
Border rows	12	20	20	22	22	24	24	26	26	28	28
Ridges	24	30	36	42	48	54	60	66	72	78	84
Shoulder stitches	7	10	10	12	12	14	14	16	16	18	18
Stitches cast off	17	22	30	34	42	48	54	58	66	70	78
Shoulder strap rows	10	12	14	16	18	20	22	24	26	28	30
Sleeve stitches	7	8	8	10	10	12	12	14	14	16	16
Sleeve rows	48	60	72	84	96	108	120	132	144	156	166

See page 35.

THE WARLEIGH SCALE FOR VESTS. No. 4.

Size	D	1	2	3	4	5	6	7	8	9	10
Stitches cast on	36	44	52	60	68	76	84	92	100	108	116
Margin stitches	8	8	8	8	12	12	12	12	16	16	16
Rows ribbed in *fours*	60	72	84	96	108	120	132	144	156	168	180
Ribs on the right side	3	4	5	6	6	7	8	9	9	10	11
Shoulder stitches	8	10	10	12	12	14	14	16	16	18	18
Stitches cast off	20	24	32	36	44	48	56	60	68	72	80
Shoulder strap rows	12	12	14	16	18	20	22	24	26	28	30

See page 35.

THE WARLEIGH SCALE FOR MITTENS.

Size	0	1	2	3	4	5	6	7	8	9	10
Stitches cast on	14	14	16	18	18	20	22	22	24	26	26
	14	14	16	18	18	20	22	22	24	26	26
	12	16	16	16	20	20	20	24	24	24	28
Total	40	44	48	52	56	60	64	68	72	76	80
Wrist rounds ribbed	34	36	38	40	42	44	46	48	50	52	54
Plain rounds	10	12	12	14	14	16	16	18	18	20	20
Thumb stitches	16	16	18	20	22	24	26	28	30	32	34
Thumb rounds	24	24	27	30	33	36	39	42	45	48	51
Number of stitches	56	60	66	72	78	84	90	96	102	108	114
Gusset stitches	6	6	6	8	8	10	10	12	12	14	14
Plain rounds	8	8	8	8	10	10	10	10	12	12	12
Rounds ribbed	8	10	10	10	12	12	12	12	14	14	14

See page 30.

THE WARLEIGH SCALE FOR CUFFS.

Size	1	2	3	4	5	6	7	8
Stitches cast on	12	14	14	16	18	18	20	22
	12	14	14	16	18	18	20	22
	12	12	16	16	16	20	20	20
Total	36	40	44	48	52	56	60	64
Rounds ribbed	44	46	48	50	52	54	56	58

See page 43.

THE WARLEIGH SCALE FOR HOODS. No. 2.

	Dolls.			Girls.					
Size	1	2	3	1	2	3	4	5	6
Stitches cast on	32	41	50	80	89	98	107	116	125
Patterns cast on	10	13	16	26	29	32	35	38	41
Hem rows	6	8	10	16	18	20	22	24	26
Headpiece rows	26	28	30	42	44	46	48	50	52
Side stitches	10	13	16	28	31	34	37	40	43
Middle stitches	12	15	18	24	27	30	33	36	39
Curtain side stitches	10	13	16	19	22	25	28	31	34
Number of stitches	32	41	50	62	71	80	89	98	107
Curtain rows	10	12	14	22	24	26	28	30	32
Border rows	6	8	10	16	18	20	22	24	26

See page 52.

BY THE SAME AUTHORESS AND PUBLISHERS.

No. 2.

FULL DIRECTIONS AND SCALES

FOR

KNITTING GLOVES,

Babies' and Dolls things, Petticoats, Capes, Throatlets, Waist Bands, Cricket Girdle, Soles, Etc.

OVER 170 PATTERNS, SIZES AND SORTS.

No. 3.

FULL DIRECTIONS

FOR

KNITTING EDGINGS,

Circles, Repeating Designs, Squares, Insertions, Etc., for Shawls Doileys, Curtains, Etc.

OVER 150 PATTERNS, SIZES AND SORTS.

PRICE ONE SHILLING EACH

www.ingramcontent.com/pod-product-compliance
Lightning Source LLC
Chambersburg PA
CBHW020150170426
43199CB00010B/965